The Great Trade Hack:
How Trump's Trade War Fails and the World Moves on

CEPR PRESS

Centre for Economic Policy Research
187 boulevard Saint-Germain | 75007, Paris, France
2 Coldbath Square | London, EC1R 5HL, UK

Email: cepr@cepr.org
Web: www.cepr.org

ISBN: 978-1-912179-92-3

The Great Trade Hack:
How Trump's Trade War Fails and the World Moves on

Richard Baldwin
IMD Business School, Lausanne

CENTRE FOR
ECONOMIC
POLICY
RESEARCH

Contents

Executive Summary

On 2 April 2025, President Donald Trump launched a sweeping tariff offensive that shook the foundations of global trade. What was the president trying to do?

The Great Trade Hack argues that Trump's actions should not be thought of as trade policy. His goal was to "hack" the world trade system in the sense of a software hack. He was trying to breach the trade system's firewall, and brute-force a quick fix using tariffs that were big, bold, and everywhere at once.

The "Grievance Doctrine": Emotion, not economics

Why was the president doing this? This book argues that we should not think of the Hack as trade policy but rather as vengeance. Economically, the tariffs are riddled with contradictions. But at an emotional level, they make perfect sense.

This is because Trump's tariffs are driven by grievance, what the book calls the "Grievance Doctrine". Think of the Grievance Doctrine as the Hack's source code – the key to unlocking what the Hack is, how it works, and where it goes next.

The Grievance Doctrine is based on a myth of betrayal, humiliation, and wreckage. Of how America played by the rules and got played. Of how the middle class got gutted while the globalist elite got rich. Trump's Hack is payback time.

According to the Doctrine, Trump's April 2nd tariffs aimed to stop the steal by rebalancing trade, to end the humiliation by reindustrialising America, to protect the struggling middle class, and to extract retribution on the thieving foreigners.

Economic reality: Why tariffs fail

Marshalling the best available evidence and economic logic, the book shows that the April 2nd tariffs cannot achieve these aims:

- **Tariffs cannot fix the trade deficit**. The trade imbalance results from Americans spending more than they produce. In a full employment economy, tariffs cannot sustainably boost production or reduce overall spending. At least not without triggering a recession. And even then, the fix is temporary.

- **Tariffs cannot revive manufacturing**. Restoring industrial strength requires coordinated, long-term investments, skilled workers, and world-class infrastructure. Tariffs provide none of these – in fact, they damage American manufacturers by raising input costs and disrupting supply chains.

- **Tariffs cannot help the middle class**. Tariffs protect the small share (under 10%) of middle-class workers in goods-producing sectors. The remaining 90% work in services, which tariffs do not shield. For them, tariffs simply increase the cost of living.

What tariffs can do, however, is damage the multilateral trade system that has underpinned global prosperity since World War II.

Political economy: Why American protectionism will persist

Why, then, do tariffs persist despite their economic failures? The book introduces the concept of "policy placebos" to explain this paradox. Tariffs persist precisely because they fail economically, yet succeed politically. They provide symbolic relief, project toughness, and shift blame onto external actors without confronting difficult domestic policy challenges like higher taxes or expanded social programmes.

The Great Trade Hack shows that protectionism is no longer an episodic deviation in American politics. Instead, it has become structurally embedded, dating back to the bipartisan embrace of anti-globalism after the 2008 financial crisis. Trump intensified the hostility in 2018. Biden softened the tone but maintained much of the tariff framework, entrenching the protectionism loop.

Global consequences: risks and scenarios

The global implications are stark. By violating key World Trade Organization principles like non-discrimination and tariff bindings, Trump's tariffs risk cascading protectionism worldwide. Historical parallels, such as the 1930 Smoot-Hawley Tariff disaster, illustrate these dangers.

The book outlines three possible scenarios:

- *Managed Multilateral Drift*, where regional agreements and WTO-compliant measures help maintain the system, though weakened.

- *Fighting Trade Blocs*, with geopolitical frictions fragmenting global commerce into competing economic blocs, weakening the WTO further.

- *Reglobalisation Without America*, where new leadership coalitions ("leadership herds") revive and strengthen the WTO around critical 21st-century issues, leaving America marginalised.

How world leaders can save the system

Given these challenges, the book provides clear recommendations for world leaders:

- **Observe and plan**: Anticipate the structural persistence of US protectionism and adjust policies, accordingly, preparing for prolonged disruption.

- **Legal discipline**: Prioritise WTO-consistent measures for retaliation, dispute resolution, and trade defence instruments to uphold rules-based trade and minimise escalation.

- **Prudent negotiation**: Maintain diplomatic channels and engage with the US and other major economies cautiously, avoiding aggressive counter-escalation that could destabilise markets.

- **Keep doors open**: Retain pathways for potential US re-engagement and prepare diplomatically for eventual shifts in US trade policy, fostering an environment conducive to reintegration.

- **Institutional renewal via leadership herds**: Form agile, issue-specific coalitions to actively renew and reform global trade governance, updating WTO disciplines to effectively address digital trade, climate policies, and other modern challenges.

Trump's April 2nd tariffs – the Great Trade Hack – marked the beginning of the post-American-leadership era, an era where American anti-globalism will live beyond President Trump.

The global trading system must now adapt, finding new forms of collective leadership. Coordinated international action is critical to safeguarding economic stability and global prosperity. Ultimately, the system's survival depends on policymakers worldwide stepping forward to maintain and evolve the rules-based global order. If it works, it will feel like diligence, not triumph.

Prologue: No disaster yet

This eBook went to press on 16 May 2025. Between that date and the main text's finalisation ten days earlier, there has been mostly good news for the world trade system. This prologue – and subsequent updates – fold in the new developments with some reflection on what they mean for the book's main messages.

The good news is that it looks less likely that the world is rushing into a 1930s spiral of tit-for-tat tariffs and collapsing trade volumes. No other nation has followed America into wanton abandonment of world trade rules. The rules-based system survives since the other countries are following the rules – or at least trying to.

To see that these recent developments *are* good news, we need to carefully interpret what happened. Not unexpectedly, the events unfolded like an episode of a reality TV series. Let's call the phases: The strike, the pain, the climbdown, and the rebrand.

- The strike.

As noted in the main text of this eBook, on 9 April Trump backed down from his April 2nd position in order to stem the financial market crisis that was brewing. He put US tariffs down to 10% for all nations except China, whose tariffs stayed at a business-destroying 145%. This prompted an equally punishing Chinese retaliation of 125% against America goods.

- The pain.

The high bilateral US-China tariffs severely and immediately disrupted US imports from China. Since US industry and consumers are so reliant on Chinese goods, that disruption was, by early May, causing US factory slowdowns, shutdowns and layoffs, along with rising prices and headlines about further hikes at Walmart, Amazon, and other mass retailers.

- The climbdown.

Given the domestic damage and growing push back from American firms and consumers, Trump needed an excuse to reduce his 145% tariffs. But he wanted China to ask for it. China refused, saying that they would not be bullied (as they had been in the 19th century) and stating that the US should lower its tariffs before any talks.

By 10 May, this you-ask-first standoff had ended with Trump caving and unilaterally announcing that the US would lower tariffs to 80% or so, even before talks began.

This gave China the face-save that it needed to start negotiations. After just two days of these talks, on the weekend of 12 May, the two sides announced a deal.

On 12 May, both sides lowered tariffs by 115%, leaving 10% each way – in addition to any tariffs that existed before 2 April (these included 20% fentanyl tariffs put in place during the first weeks of Trump's presidency and the Chinese retaliation against those).

Here is the US-China tariff timeline in a table (numbers refer to percentage points).

US tariff change.	Date.	China tariff change.	Date.
+34%	2 April	+34%	4 April
+50%	8 April	+50%	9 April
+41%	9 April	+41%	11 April
= +125%		= +125%	
-115%	12 May	-115%	12 May

In short, what started as the Chinese part of Trump's Great Trade Hack of the whole world ended with Trump taking back the whole of his China's add-on. The initial 34% on China, namely 10% base plus 24% add-on due to their large bilateral surplus, turned to 10%. Moreover, he accepted that China would maintain an equivalent retaliatory rate against American goods of 10%.

Accepting 10% for China and 10% Chinese retaliation was a near total climbdown by President Trump. The 2 April tariff formula was based on bilateral deficits, and China accounts for about a quarter of the total. Going to 10% for China demolished the coherence of Trump's April 2nd Great Trade Hack. Accepting China's 10% retaliation, after saying no retaliation would be accepted, was a further blow.

The 12 May deal was a victory for China since it forced Trump to treat China the same as countries with whom the US ran a trade surplus, not a trade deficit. It also showed that the US was desperate for a deal since these sorts of talks usually take weeks, months, or years. The fact that it was done in a weekend, and finalised without any notable Chinese concession, acted like a US distress flare that all the world could see.

This was a major loss of face for the US. It was also, potentially, a critical loss of negotiating leverage with those other nations who had watched Trump fold so fast.

• The rebrand.

Naturally, President Trump spun the US-China deal very differently. He claimed it was proof that he could get results that previous Presidents hadn't. But that claim may falter if the dozens of promised deals during the 90-day pause follow the same pattern as the UK and China deals. Reading between the lines, this led to a rebranding of the whole 90-day pause exercise.

On 16 May 2025 – perhaps to avoid similar situations in the future – Trump announced that the US would unilaterally set new tariff rates on many of its trading partners rather than striking deals with them. Specifically, the President, speaking at an unrelated meeting in the UAE, said that the new tariff rates would come "over the next two to three weeks", through letters from his administration that would inform nations what "they'll be paying to do business in the United States."

1　The Great Trade Hack

Grievance, chaos, and America's war on the system it built

On 2 April 2025, the world woke to a jarring spectacle. The nation that had spent decades building the open global trading system was torching it – on live TV. The architect had become the arsonist.

America's trade war had begun, but it looked more like an American war on trade.

Allies watched in disbelief. Rivals watched with glee. Markets shuddered. Companies scrambled. The shock was both disorienting and depressing.

President Trump's tariffs were sweeping, steep, and severe. They instantly conjured the spectre of the 1930 Smoot-Hawley Tariff, the Great Depression, and global trade collapse.

Remember what you were doing that first week of April. Your grandchildren will study it as a pivotal moment in post-WWII history.

But what was President Trump trying to do?

The Great Trade Hack

He was trying to hack the global trade system. Not reform it. Not rebuild it. Hack it – in the tech-world sense. Bypass the code, short-circuit the rules, and brute-force a quick-fix using tariffs that were big, bold, and everywhere at once.

What's the thinking behind the Hack? At its core, the Hack isn't guided by traditional ways of thinking about trade policy. It's driven by something deeper: grievance.

Let's call it "The Grievance Doctrine."

The Grievance Doctrine is a mythic tale that comes with a moral and a mission. A trusting America played by the rules and got played by globalists abroad and betrayed by globalists at home. America was humiliated. The middle class paid the price. The Doctrine is a mandate to "stop the steal" and erase the humiliation through retaliation, coercion, and the unapologetic exercise of American might.

Here's how Trump described it in the April 2nd speech that launched the Hack:

> *"For decades, our country has been looted, pillaged, raped and plundered by nations near and far, both friend and foe alike. American steelworkers, auto workers, farmers and skilled craftsmen...watched in anguish as foreign leaders have stolen our jobs, foreign cheaters have ransacked our factories, and foreign scavengers have torn apart our once beautiful American dream."*
>
> *— President Trump, 2 April 2025, White House*

The Grievance Doctrine lens brings clarity to what otherwise seems like chaos.

- Trade policy is a battlefield of betrayal and revenge.

- Allies aren't partners; they're freeloaders.

- Rules aren't stabilisers; they're handcuffs agreed by the globalist traitors.

- Trade negotiations aren't about mutual gains; they're about extracting reparations.

And you can see why tariffs are the all-purpose weapon in this trade war. Tariffs stop the steal by balancing the trade deficit. They redress the humiliation by reindustrialising America. They extract reparations from the wrong-doers, and they show that America is finally standing up for the middle class. All this while filling the US Treasury with taxes paid by foreigners. The elite's outrage is a bonus. The howls of globalist are music to MAGA ears.

What does this mean for the rest of the world?

The Grievance Doctrine channels America's sense of victimhood into trade policy that is emotionally coherent but poses huge threats to the rest of the world. If Trump gets his way, the MAGA-fied world trade system will be a US-led hierarchy of trade relations that run on power, loyalty, and tribute.

This non-system system has no shared rules, since it is entirely transactional. Trade deals are foreign submission, so every country is treated differently, and every agreement can be reopened at any time. Predictability is weakness. Volatility is a strength. The trade balance is the scorecard for national power and pride. There is no need for America to talk with trade partners about reforming the system since tearing down the old one will establish the new one.

Why this book?

This is not just another book complaining about Donald Trump. I have watched and written about trade policy for 40 years – including a stint in the George Bush Sr. White House during America's last trade war (with Japan). To me, Trump's Hack looks like a tipping point in post-war history.

Since WWII, the trade system has been the exoskeleton of global prosperity. Trade crises came and went. Negotiations broke down and resumed. Protectionism flared, but the rules-based multilateral system endured. Trump's Hack has the potential to change that.

What happens next lies in the hand of global leaders. They face a stark choice. Think of it like the choice facing players when the referee leaves the field during an amateur soccer game. The players can start arguing and fighting, or they can keep playing and start self-refereeing. The world trade system has just seen the referee go walkabout. The future of global trade will depend on whether the rest of the world (i) continues to play by the rules or (ii) descend into 1930s style chaos marked by tariff vigilantism and chaotic retaliation.

I am optimistic. The US accounts for 15% of world trade. I believe that the nations responsible for the other 85% will defend the rules-based system that has underpinned human prosperity for so long. But the 1930s scenario is a real possibility. There are plenty of tensions in the rest of the world, including conflict between the EU and China, that could trigger Grievance Doctrine-like reactions beyond the US.

The next few months will, I believe, go down in the books as one of history's turning points. Policy windows like this are rare and short. If ever there was a time to step back, survey the damage, and think clearly about what's actually happening, and what might come next, that time is now.

The book's goals

My book's first goal is to offer a cohesive explanation of the "whats, hows and whys" behind Trump's trade war. The main takeaway is this: Trump's trade war is grievance in action – victimhood weaponised and unleashed as tariffs. It's not economic strategy; it's MAGA-fied trade policy, where protectionism becomes a form of emotional retribution without a great deal of thought about the consequences. Not at all unlike Brexit.

The second goal is to show that Trump's tariffs will not work the way he thinks they will. I show why tariffs can't rebuild the US middle class, reindustrialise America, or balance its trade deficit. Not won't. I mean can't. Trump's Hack will also fail when it comes to the US–China conflict due to the Hack's fatal flaw on this score. It confuses a "system clash" for a trade war. It is trying to use tariffs to fight a clash that can only be managed, not won.

Since tariffs cannot fix the middle-class malaise, and that malaise is driving protectionism, both will persist. Even if President Trump stepped down tomorrow, the hostility to trade would continue – trade hesitancy/hostility is the mainstream view on both sides of the aisle in Washington. We all have to get used to a trade system that is post-American leadership.

The third goal of the book is to identify the damage done to the rules-based multilateral system, and the fourth is to discuss what the rest of the world should do to guard the system and avoid a repeat of the 1930s.

Why an instant book?

I have written an instant book since the consequences of the "Great Trade Hack" are unfolding fast and we don't know where they are heading. Trump's Hack has raised the spectre of the Great Depression and global trade collapse. The most pressing priority is to make sure that the spectre does not turn into a reality.

I'm an optimist. I don't think this will happen, but it is important to be alive to the possibility. Trade wars, like real wars, can spin out of control.

What this book is not

This book is not a dismissal of the goals of the Great Trade Hack. American middle-class malaise is real and has been since the upheaval caused by automation and globalisation in the 1990s. Something needs be done. I don't believe that Trump's Hack is that "thing". But who knows, maybe the Hack will work. That would be a good thing for America.

Who is it written for?

The book is written for a wide audience: policymakers, business leaders, journalists, and concerned non-specialists, but scholars not so much. This is not an academic moment.

The book's structure

The book comes in four parts. The first part (Chapters 2 and 3) lays out my diagnosis of why America launched the Hack now and why it has been so chaotically managed. The second part (Chapters 4 and 5) debunks the myth that tariffs can fix trade deficits, reindustrialise America, or help the middle class. Part three turns to a systemic framing of the hack and its and global consequences (Chapters 6 and 7). The fourth part (Chapters 8 and 9) is forward looking. The final chapter (Chapter 10) sketches a way forward and discusses what world leaders should be doing now to avoid America's recklessness in 2025 ruining global prosperity, as American recklessness did in 1930.

2 The Grievance Doctrine

Grievance explains US protectionism and why it'll outlasts Trump

US trade policy has gone rogue, puzzling traditional allies and competitors alike. What happened to the architect of the rules-based global trade system – the one-time champion of open markets and predictability? Today, erratic tariff policy, hostility to multilateral institutions, and performative brinkmanship have become the norm.

Around the world, policymakers and observers are asking themselves: Why is America acting this way?

This chapter argues that the answer is not "because Donald Trump was elected president". President Trump is a culmination, not an aberration, in my view. The radical change we have all watched is the outcome of a much longer story. A systemic failure that has quietly undermined middle-class living standards.

For decades, US policymakers have shied away from the social policies that cushion workers in other advanced economies. Things like durable unemployment insurance, active labour market support, relocation and retraining schemes, and regional adjustment funds. The middle classes in every other advanced economy in the world take these sharing-and-caring policies for granted.

But in Washington, such policies are off the table and anti-globalisation is the default alternative. Protection offers the appearance of action. It is visible, forceful, and wrapped in the language of fairness.

The sad part is that the tariffs Donald Trump has imposed will not, indeed logically cannot, redress the middle-class malaise. Tariffs can help workers in goods-producing sectors, but less than 10% of the American middle class have jobs in such sectors. Most of them have service-sector jobs, and it is impossible to put tariffs on imported services.

This is why tariffs should not be thought of as part of a real solution for middle-class malaise. They are policy placebos, not policy. Tariffs allow politicians to shift blame from domestic policy failures to foreign scapegoats. Tariffs tell voters that their problems are made in China, Mexico, or Europe.

I flesh out my argument by following a trail of questions:

- Why is the American middle class so angry?

- Why did this lead to a backlash?

- Why was the backlash so protectionist?

- Why does Trump think the US is victim (the Grievance Doctrine)?

- Why can't tariffs help the middle class?

- Why will protectionism persist even though it doesn't work?

Why is America's middle class so angry?

Drive through any town in the Rust Belt and you'll see the boarded-up shops and abandoned factories. The police officers carrying naloxone injectors to reverse opioid overdoses.

The anger simmering in America's middle class isn't irrational – it's rooted in lived experience. Many families can no longer dream of affording the homes they grew up in, and job security feels like a relic of the past. Middle-class incomes no longer sustain a middle-class life.

But it is not just about the prices they pay and how much is in their wallets. Pride matters. The last few decades have wounded the pride and shaken the confidence of many working Americans for whom the American Dream was disrupted – especially those who didn't go to university, but even many who did. Recent analysis by the Pew Research Center illustrates the recent socioeconomic woes of the US middle class, but also how the American Dream wasn't always an empty slogan.[1]

The American Dream is not a promise that you'll do well. It is a belief. It is a hope. It's the idea that working hard, showing up every day and giving it your best, will allow anyone – regardless of background – to build a better life for their families. Part of the dream was a belief that, regardless of the nature of the shocks and shifts, you'd have a fighting chance of being one of the winners.

From FDR's helping hand to Reagan's trickle down

The American Dream was underpinned by a collective belief set in place by Franklin D. Roosevelt's New Deal policies. Government had a duty to help ordinary people navigate economic hardship and build better lives. Government was there to help the little guy – to look after economic stability, full employment, and basic welfare. To fight cartels and break up monopolies. That's when Social Security and unemployment insurance were invented. Unions and collective bargaining were legalised, protected, and encouraged. The Fair Labor Standards Act put a floor on workplace conditions.

FDR's policies marked a decisive break from the hands-off, pro-business approach of his predecessor, President Calvin Coolidge. FDR substituted the Coolidge concensus (laissez-faire capitalism) with a new consensus (an active government committed to economic security and social justice).

But that consensus began to erode in the 1980s. Ronald Reagan's presidency marked a sharp ideological pivot. His supply-side economics and "trickle-down" theory recast the government not as a guardian of fairness, but as a barrier to growth. When Reagan took office in 1981, the top marginal income tax rate stood at about 70%. Within a decade, it

---

1   Kochhar, R. (2024, May 31). The state of the American middle class. Pew Research Center. https://www.pewresearch.org/race-and-ethnicity/2024/05/31/the-state-of-the-american-middle-class/

had been slashed to under 40% – a level it has hovered around ever since, regardless of whether Democrats or Republicans have held the reins.

This wasn't just a change in fiscal policy and tax cuts. It was a transformation of political philosophy. The national narrative shifted – from a government that helped the little guy to one where the little guys were expected to help themselves. Collective welfare gave way to individual responsibility. The social compact was rewritten, subtly but profoundly, to favour markets over public provision. This new consensus held through the Biden years, not because it was explicitly endorsed by the left but because it had become the received wisdom in US mainstream political discourse.

The economic impact of this policy shift was not massive up to the mid-1980s There were shocks but they hit all elements of society equally. The oil shocks of the 1970s and subsequent stagflation meant hard times for everyone.

When the globotics shocks landed on inadequate social policy

When the twin bombs of globalisation and automation landed, all that changed. (In my 2019 book, *The Globotics Upheaval*, I call the combination the "globotics shocks"; globotics = globalisation + robotics).[2]

The ICT revolution accelerated industrial automation from the 1970s and turbocharged globalisation from the late 1980s. ICT was the source of the globotics shocks. The economic impact of this combined shock caused massive labour force dislocation in all advanced economies. The globotics shocks revealed the vulnerability created by the FDR-to-Reagan shift.

Other advanced economies responded to these shocks with expanded social programmes and policies to help workers adjust to automation and import competition. But in the US, workers faced these shocks all on their own. Free-market forces did little to smooth the transitions to the new economy that the globotics shocks had created.

The uneven impact

But the impact of the shock and lack of helping-hand policies had very different effects on Americans who worked with hands on tools and those worked with hands on keyboard.

Manual workers suffered. As I explain in my 2016 book, *The Great Convergence*, American manual workers were hit hard by both aspects of the globotics shocks.[3] Let's start with the robots. The ICT revolution, which began in 1973 with the invention of computers-on-a-chip, transformed industrial automation. It turned factory robots into increasingly capable and cost-effective substitutes for human labour. Tasks that once required a skilled machinist or assembly-line worker could now be done faster, cheaper,

2   Baldwin, R. (2019). *The globotics upheaval: Globalization, robotics, and the future of work.* Weidenfeld & Nicolson.
3   Baldwin, R. E. (2016). *The great convergence: Information technology and the new globalization.* Harvard University Press.

and more reliably by machines. As automation advanced, many solid, middle-class jobs were automated away.

Globalisation made things worse for US factory workers. China and other low-wage exporters were selling the same products that American factory workers were making but for much less. This reduced the number of manufacturing jobs even further. Import competition, in other words, amplified the robot-driven gutting of US factory jobs.

All this was accelerated by offshoring. Up until the globotics shocks, the US industrial base was built on dense, local production ecosystems. Firms, workers, suppliers, and know-how clustered in places like Detroit, Cleveland, and Pittsburgh. But once ICT made it possible to coordinate complex production activities across international borders, US firms began slicing up their supply chains and relocating pieces abroad. ICT made it feasible; wage gaps made it irresistible.

Critically, offshoring wasn't just about chasing cheap labour. American companies exported not just jobs, but capabilities and technology. In moving factories overseas, they transferred US know-how, tooling, and capital to foreign affiliates – effectively arming low-wage workers in developing countries with high-end technology. American workers found themselves in a lopsided competition: high tech and high wages at home versus high-tech, low-wage labour abroad.

At first, the offshored tasks were simple – shoe stitching, toy assembly. But over time, more complex and skilled tasks followed. Toolmakers, component suppliers, and specialised craftspeople lost contracts, customers, and eventually their livelihoods. The tightly woven industrial fabric of American manufacturing began to unravel. In short, America's industrial base was eroded passively in reaction to automation and globalisation. But it was actively eroded by US firms shipping jobs and factories to low-wage nations. This was called the Global Value Chain Revolution.[4]

The result was a three-pincher middle-class squeeze. Automation replaced them, globalisation undercut them, and offshoring displaced them. Wages fell. Millions of jobs disappeared. Factory towns were gutted economically and socially. Main streets emptied, futures dimmed, and a quiet despair displaced pride and hope.

While globotics put factory workers through the wringer, it turned high-education workers into winners.

High-education service workers thrived. Those in knowledge-intensive jobs, and the education to get them, benefited from the ICT Revolution. For them, it wasn't about substitution – it was augmentation.

ICT didn't replace white-collar professionals, it supercharged them. Accountants got spreadsheets. Designers got CAD software. Lawyers got searchable databases. Managers

---

4   World Trade Organization. (2013). World Trade Report 2013: Factors shaping the future of world trade (Chapter C: The role of trade in global production). WTO.

got real-time dashboards. Consultants got instant access to global information. The digital revolution took tasks that once required hours or days and compressed them into minutes. With better tools, skilled workers could do more, faster, and with greater precision – and that made them more valuable.

Just as important, most of the tasks they performed were in non-tradable sectors. You can't outsource a meeting with a doctor. So, while manufacturing jobs were being sent overseas, replaced by robots, or faced stiff import competition, the jobs in finance, education, healthcare, legal services, and high-end consulting stayed put.

In short, the ICT revolution twisted the American Dream along with the American economy. Those with degrees soared. Those without watched from the sidelines, wondering why a country built on opportunity had left them behind.

Why did this lead to a backlash in America?

While the same globotics shock hit every advanced economy hard, and forced broadly similar skills twists, the magnitude and duration of the American middle-class suffering is in a class by itself.

Socioeconomic unravelling of a once-secure middle class

The economic gutting of America's middle class didn't just show up in the unemployment lines or stagnant wage charts – it tore through the social fabric in ways never before seen in a rich country.

The fallout was brutal. Communities once held together by steady jobs and shared prosperity began to fray. The US experienced a surge of social pathologies that set it apart from other advanced economies: frequent school shootings, an opioid crisis that ravaged entire regions, an obesity epidemic fuelled by stress and poor nutrition, and widespread medical bankruptcies in a system that ties healthcare to employment.

The damage went deeper. America recorded shockingly high maternal mortality rates, crushing levels of student debt, the highest incarceration rate in the developed world, and staggering levels of old-age poverty and homelessness. Among white, working-class Americans in particular, suicide rates rose sharply – along with what economists Anne Case and Angus Deaton have called "deaths of despair". They are signs of more than just rising inequality. They are signs of social collapse in a nation that allowed its middle class to be hollowed out.

No other advanced economy exhibits this depth or breadth of social pain. As Case and Deaton document in *Deaths of Despair and the Future of Capitalism*,[5] America's social unravelling is not an accident. It is the predictable result of a system that delivered prosperity to the few and precarity to the many.

5 Case, A. & Deaton, A. (2020). Deaths of Despair and the Future of Capitalism. Princeton University Press.

To add insult to injury, while their woes were accumulating, they were forced to witness their relative standing decline. The rich pulled away from them on the upscale side, while the poor caught up on the downscale side – as the *Financial Times* columnist John Burn-Murdoch showed in his Data Points column[6]. If you think about that, you'll see that it meant that the American Dream was working – just not for the middle class.

Should we blame globalisation and robots for middle-class malaise?

While the globotics shock hit every advanced economy hard, the lack of effective social policies left the American middle class uniquely unprepared for the globotics disruptions.

Unlike Canada and most European nations, the United States entered the era of globalisation, automation, and offshoring without the social scaffolding needed to protect its middle class. It lacked universal healthcare, which meant that losing a job often meant losing medical coverage exactly when you and your family were going through hard times. It offered only weak unemployment insurance, with limited duration, leaving many families vulnerable to income shocks.

The US also failed to provide paid parental leave or affordable childcare, making it harder for working families, and especially women, to stay in the labour force as the economy shifted from factories to offices.

Higher education, which should have been a gateway to new opportunities, was increasingly priced out of reach, forcing young people into crushing student debt just to keep pace with job market demands. Nor were there systematic policies to help workers retrain and relocate to new jobs. While European nations invested heavily in active labour market policies, including effective job placement services and apprenticeships, US efforts in this area were underfunded, fragmented, and poorly targeted.

The government of other rich nations saw it as their duty to lend a helping hand, and to grow the government and tax bases to make this possible. In the US, low taxes and small government was the mantra. That's why the middle class faced the globotics shock alone.

The absence of social protection made all the difference. What turned out to be manageable transitions in other countries became life-altering disruptions for the American middle class. Other nations saw problems, but not on this scale.

Why was the backlash so protectionist?

While the backlash and election of a populist is understandable given the length of the fail-trail traditional politicians have left behind themselves, the question remains: Why is today's populist so anti-trade? In part the answer is: Why not?

6   Burn-Murdoch, J. (2025, January 3). Inequality hasn't risen. Here's why it feels like it has. Financial Times. https://www. ft.com/content/b325af8f-1864-448e-9b3e-bd1a18333a08

Populism is a shallow political philosophy. The touchstone is a simple mantra: the people are pure; the elite are corrupt, so elect me and I promise to [this space is left blank on purpose].

Any policy suits as long as it can be portrayed as something the elite has not been doing – especially if the fill-in-the-blank policy would outrage the elite. The point is that populism is driven by anger – not a careful study of what made the people angry, or what policies would address their plight. At various times in living memory and in various countries, the fill-in-the-blank policy ranged from far left to far right – from fascism, communism, and the Cultural Revolution to Brexit and extreme anti-immigration promises.

Trump's love affair with tariffs

The direct source of the anti-trade bias is simpler. The deeply held convictions of the president. This is striking.

Donald Trump is not a man troubled by the hobgoblin that Ralph Waldo Emerson was referring to when he said: "consistency is the hobgoblin of little minds". He has been pro- and anti-gun control, pro- and anti-choice, pro- and anti-Hillary Clinton, and he has even been both a Democrat and a Republican. But the one hobgoblin he has held on to all along is the near-magical promise of tariffs.

In the 1980s, as a private businessman, Trump took out full-page advertisements in major newspapers to criticise US tariff liberalisation.[7] In the ads, you can see how even back when America was great – as in "Make America Great Again" – he believed that the US was being treated unfairly in international trade.

President Trump channels the middle-class rage into an anti-globalism. His thinking and that of those around him has not really been pulled together. There is no single document that lays out a coherent plan or philosophy. The *Project 2025* playbook offers some clues.[8] The document includes a chapter on trade authored by presidential advisor Peter Navarro. The chapter's tone is polemical, echoing the sorts of zingers that fill Donald Trump's speeches., but is not a plan.

Why does Trump think the US is victim? The Grievance Doctrine

To fully understand why the populist backlash took such a strongly protectionist form under Trump, you need to look beyond economics. At its heart, Trump's trade policy isn't guided by traditional economic logic or strategic international relations.

In my view, it's guided by rage, not reason. And this explains why "erratic" and "chaotic" are terms that are so often applied to President Trump's trade policy. To many observers, the pattern is that there is no pattern. No joined-up strategy, no vision, no framework.

7   Viser, M. (2025, April 9). Trump's long history hating global trade – and loving tariffs. The Washington Post. https://www.washingtonpost.com/politics/2025/04/09/trump-tariffs-history-stock-market/

8   Navarro, P. (2023). Make America First Again in Trade and Manufacturing Policy. In Mandate for Leadership: The Conservative Promise (pp. 397-408). The Heritage Foundation. https://www.project2025.org

But I think I have found a blueprint implicit in a 2016 Trump speech[9] and the president's 2025 trade policy agenda.[10] Let's call it the "Grievance Doctrine," which is based on coherence guided by emotions rather than economic, or International Relations 101.

What is the Grievance Doctrine? It is a tale with a morale. A trusting America played by the rules and got played by foreigners. The Doctrine is a mandate to stop the steal and get even coercing concessions from trade partners.

Once you start by looking at Trump's seemingly erratic trade policy though the lens of the Grievance Doctrine, everything starts to make sense.

- Trade policy is a battlefield of betrayal and revenge.

- Tariffs aren't taxes; they're punishments.

- Trade deficits aren't macroeconomic outcomes; they're theft.

- Allies aren't partners; they're freeloaders.

- Rules aren't stabilisers; they're handcuffs.

- Trade negotiations are about the tribute that foreigners will offer.

To understand the Doctrine, you must cast off your traditional thinking about the goals of trade policy. It isn't any of the usual "isms" that have classified trade policy regimes over the centuries. It is not a liberalism, mercantilism, protectionism, nationalism, and certainly not free-trade-ism. It's more primal. This of it as institutionalised indignation.

The Doctrine's "origin story"

Every worldview needs a story of how things went wrong and how they can be fixed. Trump's trade doctrine begins with a foundational tale of betrayal – simple, emotionally powerful, and politically effective.

In the Grievance Doctrine's origin story, foreign companies won because they cheated, not because they were more competitive. They closed their markets; the US opened its. They used exchange rates to undercut US domestic and export sales. They stole intellectual property, subsidised industries, and deployed all manner of regulatory trickery. China is the cheater-in-chief, according to the Grievance Doctrine. It is a predatory state that weaponised the rules-based multilateral system.

American leaders sold out the middle class to make a buck. The American elite profited from the cheating. Donald Trump, in his 28 June 2016 speech in Pennsylvania, stated: "Hillary Clinton unleashed a trade war against the American worker when she supported one terrible trade deal after another – from NAFTA to China to South Korea."

9   TIME. (2016, June 28). Read Donald Trump's Speech on Trade. https://time.com/4386335/donald-trump-trade-speech-transcript/
10 U.S. Trade Representative. (2025). The President's 2025 Trade Policy Agenda. https://ustr.gov/sites/default/files/files/reports/2025/President%20Trump's%202025%20Trade%20Policy%20Agenda.pdf

The list of traitors includes pro-trade Republicans and Democrats, trade diplomats, economists, think-tankers and other members of the free-trade mafia. These globalists sold out workers, outsourced industries, and worshipped at the altar of multilateralism and Wall Street while Main Street withered.

The setting up of the rules-based multilateral system was an American surrender. Institutions like the WTO, and trade agreements like NAFTA, were concrete evidence that the globalists sacrificed American industry and American workers to make a buck. They cloaked this betrayal in free-market ideology.

The middle class paid the price for the betrayal. Middle-class problems are, in the Grievance Doctrine's origin story, the result of foreign cheating and globalist betrayal. These shattered middle-class neighbourhoods and stripped workers of the dignity. Trade deficits are symbols of this national humiliation.

The Grievance Doctrine leads to a MAGA-fied trade policy

The Doctrine casts the United States not as an empire in decline but as a superpower that was cheated. Under the Grievance Doctrine, trade policy follows an emotional imperative. It's about vengeance. It is about punishing betrayal and righting old wrongs. Left at the wayside are traditional motives like efficiency, mutual gain, or institutional predictability.

The emotional coherence dictates that trade diplomacy should be coercive rather than cooperative. It also dictates the breaking of all the agreements and promises made in the past. Those were made by American traitors while they were robbing the US middle class. Trade rules and free trade agreements are emblems of America's humiliation. Violating rules and norms is America taking back control. Careful readers will note the echoes between the Grievance Doctrine and the "Take Back Control" slogan of the Brexit referendum campaign.

In the Doctrine, tariffs are the perfect tool. Tariffs can be used to punish. When China cheats, it gets tariffed. When allies rely on US security while running trade surpluses, they get tariffed. When companies move jobs overseas, they get tariffed. Tariffs can also create leverage – pain and urgency that forces the other side to submit. Here is where the Grievance Doctrine blends with "The Art of the Deal". Trade deals happen when the other side is scared the whole thing will fall apart.

Under the Grievance Doctrine, loyalty and submission replace rules. Countries who want access to the US market have to earn it with loyalty or lucre or, preferably, both. Market access is coin-operated privilege.

This, in my view, explains a lot. Breaking rules and trade agreements is a show of strength. It is America finally standing up for the middle class.

You can see how this slots straight into "Make America Great Again". In fact, we should think of the Grievance Doctrine as MAGA-ifed trade policy.

3   Chaos: By design or dysfunction?

Why Trump's trade policy is so erratic

US trade policy under President Trump is erratic. It is chaotic. It almost seems as if it were crafted by the producer of a reality TV show inventing shocking twists to keep the binge-watching public glued to their screens..

- 3 February 2025: President Trump pauses tariffs on Mexico and Canada that he had announced just days earlier – only to reinstate and escalate them soon after.

- Early February 2025: The president imposes 10% tariffs on all Chinese imports, then doubles them to 20%, and then threatens more hikes.

- 2-9 April: In a period of 10 days, the president unilaterally announces and then reverses the most sweeping tariff policy in modern US history, without negotiating a thing. It is a one-man trade war and a one-man surrender.

Gripping drama, no doubt. But this isn't US trade policy as the world once knew it. And the show goes on.

In reality TV, no one knows how the season finale will end. In the case of reality TV, that's a feature not a bug. But when it comes to trade policy, volatility is corrosive. It poisons business investment, rattles financial markets, and destabilises the everyday planning of small businesses and working families who are living paycheque to paycheque.

This is not how trade policy worked under any past president, not even Trump in his first term. The mystery here is not the goals of Trump's trade policy, it's the chaotic way these goals are being pursued. As Chapter 2 argued, the goals follow an emotional coherence in what I called the Grievance Doctrine.

The Doctrine portrays the US as a victim of a rigged world trade system. Set up by globalist elite in the US who profited from them, the rules allowed foreign rivals to cheat. America's middle class paid the price. Now it's payback time.

The Doctrine describes the US as a victim of unfair world trade rules created by global elites for personal gain. The rules allowed foreign competitors to cheat and the result was the exploitation of America's middle class. The goals of Trump's trade policy are to stop the cheating, punish the globalists, and make foreigners pay reparation.

There is, however, nothing in the Doctrine that justifies the erratic implementation of US trade policy.

A textbook case of this erratic-ness is the way the president often suspends his announced tariffs in a way that make it seem like he is negotiating with himself. A closer look at this behaviour is revealing.

Why is Trump negotiating tariffs with himself (in public)?

Trumpian tariffs come out of the White House like bullets from a Gatling gun. Chad Bown, the ex-Chief Economist for the Department of State who tracks this closely at the Peterson Institute of International Economics in Washington, counts 51 official actions on trade in the administration's first 108 days.[1]

But many of the bullets are suspended or adjusted just after they leave the barrel. In world trade negotiations, these suspensions and adjustments are called 'concessions' to trade partners. Astoundingly, Trump has made these concessions without having won any concessions in return. In many cases, he doesn't seem to have even talked to trade partners. Looking from the outside in, the president seems to be negotiating with himself – in public.

A telling example: The 2-9 April 2025 tariff climbdowns

The evolution of the 2 April tariffs, related above, provides a telling example of historical tariffs being announced and walked back, all without obtaining foreign concessions – a classic example of self-negotiation.

It was certainly bold. The Trump administration's April 2025 tariffs were launched with the rhetorical force of a revolutionary manifesto. President Trump promised to reset the playing field, punish surplus nations, and rake in cash for America with a bold new baseline: 10% tariffs on nearly all imports, plus tailor-made hikes (some up to 50%) for countries judged insufficiently "fair". Announced on 2 April,[2] these tariffs were marketed as hardball – reciprocity, at last, with teeth.

But on 9 April, Trump suspended these tariffs for 90 days.[3] This sort of concession, or ceasefire, is common in traditional trade wars. But while the suspension wasn't unusual, the lack of foreign concessions was. Trump did not secure any matching concessions from foreign governments.

The tariffs placed on China were not included in the 9 April 2025 climbdown and had, after rounds of retaliation, reached 145%.[4]

The series of unilateral climbdowns continued on 12 April, when the administration quietly announced (on the Customs and Border Protection website, not WhiteHouse.org) an exemption from the reciprocal tariff regime for smartphones, laptops, and key

1   Bown, C. P. (2025, February 25). Trump's trade war timeline 2.0: An up-to-date guide. Peterson Institute for International Economics. https://www.piie.com/blogs/realtime-economics/2025/trumps-trade-war-timeline-20-date-guide

2   The White House. (2025, April). Fact sheet: President Donald J. Trump declares national emergency to increase our competitive edge, protect our sovereignty, and strengthen our national and economic security. https://www.whitehouse.gov/fact-sheets/2025/04/fact-sheet-president-donald-j-trump-declares-national-emergency-to-increase-our-competitive-edge-protect-our-sovereignty-and-strengthen-our-national-and-economic-security/

3   CNN Business. (2025, April 9). Trump announces 90-day pause on 'reciprocal' tariffs with exception of China. https://edition.cnn.com/2025/04/09/business/reciprocal-tariff-pause-trump/index.html

4   The New York Times. (2025, April 10). Trump has added 145% tariff to China, White House clarifies. https://www.nytimes.com/2025/04/10/business/economy/china-tariffs-145-percent.html

electronic components.[5] These exemptions applied broadly – not just to friendly nations but also to China, the primary exporter of these goods. These electronic goods and parts account for more than a quarter of Chinese exports to the US in a normal year.[6,7] The 12 April change was thus a major unilateral concession to China in the US–China trade war that Trump had started just ten days before.

This was, in effect, Trump handing China a major tariff concession – no negotiation, no summit, not even a phone call to Xi Jinping.[8] Publicly, the administration framed the move as a "temporary exclusion" due to national economic considerations.

The irony is acute. The man who built his tariff legacy on leverage and deal-making made his biggest tariff concession to China while negotiating with no one but himself. The 12 April exemptions are a perfect illustration of why traditional trade policy was so careful and so institutionalised. The backdowns show that unilateral tariff policy, when disconnected from diplomatic engagement, can become a policy of half-measures, exemptions, and backpedals.

Yes-sir advisors create a presidential "wishful thinking bubble"

The peculiarities of Trump's tariff policies appear to reflect the president's personal convictions combined with a coterie of yes-sir advisors. My theory for why he is negotiating with himself in public starts from four premises.

First, Trump loves tariffs in a way that I have not seen in any country during the 40 years I have been following trade policy. The president acts as if they were his Marvel "superpower". He has repeatedly called "tariffs" the most beautiful word in the dictionary. This deep faith in tariffs, however, is tempered by another long-standing aspect of his approach to the world: he is pragmatic, not dogmatic. That's the second premise: he does not view flexibility, even flip-flopping, as a sign of weakness.

Third, President Trump appears to live in a 'wishful thinking bubble', which is created by advisors whose main job seems to be to spotlight his brilliance. This aspect is on full display during the televised Cabinet Meetings, where the whole world witnesses one Secretary after the other testifying to the historical greatness and uniqueness of their boss. Having selected his political appointments on the basis of loyalty rather than competence, the wishful thinking bubble is a natural result.

Fourth, these advisors view it as their job to turn every wish and whisper that arises inside the wishful thinking bubble into US trade policy – and this at the speed of light. To misquote Sherlock Holmes, they are there to twist the facts to fit the tariffs.

5   CNN. (2025, April 12). Smartphones and computers are now exempt from Trump's latest tariffs. https://edition.cnn.com/2025/04/12/tech/trump-electronics-china-tariffs/index.html
6   LinkedIn. (2025, February 21). US Electronics Imports in 2024: Key Data and Insights. https://www.linkedin.com/pulse/us-electronics-imports-2024-key-data-insights-tradeimex-zbfkc
7   Tom's Hardware. (2025, April 9). Trump tariffs will hit consoles, monitors, and laptops hardest. https://www.tomshardware.com/tech-industry/trump-tariffs-will-hit-consoles-monitors-and-laptops-hardest-u-s-imports-66-percent-or-more-from-china
8   BBC. (2025, April 12). Trump exempts smartphones and computers from new tariffs. https://www.bbc.com/news/articles/c20xn626y81o

That's why, in my view, US trade policy resembles a reality show production room delivering plot twists daily. President Trump apparently gets tariff wishes pretty frequently, and they become tariff announcements at a pace that has nothing to do with the traditional, measured, reflective, consultative trade policy formulation of past presidents.

What explains the chaos – incompetence or malevolence?

The traditional approach to trade policy – developed methodically by layers of lawyers, economists, and trade diplomats – emphasised predictability, long-term stability, and careful planning.

I participated in this process when I followed trade matters for the Council of Economic Advisers under President Bush Sr. Admittedly that was a while back, but the basics of the process haven't changed much over the years. This traditional approach aimed explicitly at nurturing American manufacturing, agriculture, and mining sectors through institutional processes. In other words, predictability of means was an essential 'end' in itself.

But why is Trump's trade policy so chaotic? Among the elbow-patched Harris Tweed crowd, there are two schools of thought:

- Incredible incompetence.

- Machiavellian malevolence.

The two are not mutually exclusive; both could be part of the chaos causation. Quite plausibly, the tariff policy chaos is due to incompetence, but it is being instrumentalised by malevolent players in the Trump administration.

The case for incompetence: Three sources of tariff chaos

The chaos of Trump's second-term trade policy is apparent to all. Tariffs are announced, reversed, suspended, or doubled within days. Key partners blindsided. Supply chains whiplashed. Why the chaos?

As mentioned, some observers view this as the result of institutional incompetence, even if some of the competency seems to have been set up on purpose. From the incompetence perspective, three distinct factors fuel the chaos. I consider them in turn.

First, Trump's personal business experience – grounded in 1970s real-estate bargaining – favours unpredictability and brinkmanship as a deliberate negotiation strategy.[9] This instinctive approach, honed through years in the rough-and-tumble world of New York

---

9 Schleckser, J. (2025, March 5). Negotiating like Trump: Power, pressure, and unpredictability. Inc. https://www.inc.com/jim-schleckser/negotiating-like-trump-power-pressure-and-unpredictability/91155929

real estate, is surely one of the most important sources of the chaos we've all wondered about.

Second, Trump's reality TV experience conditions him to view tariffs as theatrical performances designed to project strength when implemented and wisdom when reversed.[10] The spectacle itself – rapid impositions followed by partial retreats – becomes the primary goal, overshadowing economic rationale and causing damaging uncertainty.

Third, institutional sabotage has systematically dismantled the careful interagency process historically responsible for evidence-based trade policy. By subordinating USTR under Commerce and filling key positions with inexperienced loyalists, Trump ensures that decisions reflect personal whims rather than national strategic interests.[11]

• A real estate negotiator meets trade policy

In real estate, the substance of the agreements matters, of course, but the main job of the lead negotiator is to extract the maximum from the other guys – or so it seems from my academic perch. That is why, in my limited understanding, negotiations in real estate often devolve into chaotic, start-stop affairs full of bluffs, brinkmanship, and theatrics, as each side manoeuvres to grab a larger slice of the pie.

But this chaos isn't accidental – it's strategic. The disorder serves to signal credibility. By appearing genuinely ready to walk away and collapse the deal, negotiators raise the stakes, forcing their counterpart to confront the prospect of losing everything. The chaos, in other words, is how negotiators demonstrate they're serious. How they convince the other guys that they may lose it all if they don't hand over a bigger slice of the pie. In Trump's case, the brinkmanship, more than once, went all the way to bankruptcy. But these were bankruptcies where others lost money without doing much damage to his own net worth.

In short, real estate taught President Trump that unpredictability and risk were integral, manageable parts of a negotiator's toolkit.

Given this background, it's no wonder that Trump's trade policies are a sharp departure from the carefully calibrated, institutionally driven trade policies of his predecessors. We should expect trade policy to seem erratic when it's run like a Manhattan property deal that just has to get the signatures on the sale.

Trump's real estate experience also taught him one simple rule: the seller is ripping off the buyer. From that premise, it's just a logic hop-skip-and-jump to the idea – which the President is firmly convinced of and which shapes his attitude towards trade – that a

---

10   Bienstock, J. (2024, May 3). The Donald Trump I saw on The Apprentice. Slate. https://slate.com/culture/2024/05/donald-trump-news-2024-trial-verdict-apprentice.html
11   Foreign Policy. (2025, April 25). The drivers (and passengers) of Trump's foreign policy. Foreign Policy. https://foreignpolicy.com/2025/04/25/trump-100-days-influential-officials-navarro-bessent-witkoff/

bilateral trade deficit is theft. Trump regularly quotes the dollar amount of America's trade deficits to quantify the size of the heist. This notion is completely false – as anyone versed in mainstream, positive-sum business practices would attest. Nevertheless, it is a cornerstone of Trump's belief system.

- ### *The Apprentice* learnings: Tariffs as performance

Later, Trump won financial rewards and personal adulation in reality television (on *The Apprentice*). Here, his financial rewards hinged explicitly on spectacle, uncertainty, and drama. Audience engagement depended upon cliffhangers, surprise decisions, and cringe-worthy personal confrontations. Stability and predictability were to be avoided at all costs!

As they say, "you can take the man out of the reality TV, but you can't take the reality out of the man." And this, I believe, helps explain the chaos. In Trumpland, tariffs aren't just policy – they are performance. Just compare, in your mind's eye, announcements made by Presidents Reagan and Obama when they were sitting behind the Roosevelt Desk to those of President Trump.

When made from the Oval Office, Trump's tariff announcements carry all the hallmarks of a staged show or marketing video. They are theatrically delivered in a way that, in my view, aims as much at public perception as at economic policy – more strut than strategy. When announced on social media, as they frequently are, they are abrupt, sensational, and perfectly timed for maximum media impact. They seem calibrated to generate turbulence, and discomfort for the elite.

The 2 April tariffs felt like a season premiere – part circus, part shock reveal, timed for prime-time attention. And it worked. I was in Tokyo at the time and lots of people stayed up till the early morning hours to watch it live. When has trade policy ever generated that sort of public attention?

The theatrics were especially evident in his escalating tariff exchanges with China – making headlines and reinforcing an image of toughness. Later, he would strategically reduce or delay tariffs, positioning himself as pragmatic and wise. Each reversal was presented not as policy inconsistency but as a magnanimous concession that only he could deliver.

This cycle of threats and concessions fits neatly into Trump's reality TV background: heighten uncertainty, boost ratings (or in this case, media attention), and then deliver a last-minute twist. Predictability and stability – long hallmarks of US trade strategy – have thus given way to improvisation and spectacle. While this may be entertaining for his MAGA base, it leaves US businesses uncertain about long-term investment decisions, and foreign governments unsure of America's true intentions.

In short, Trumpian tariffs are chaotic in part because they are not merely economic tools – his trade policy is a stage upon which he continuously reinforces his brand:

strong enough to confront, flexible enough to negotiate, and always ready to dominate the headlines.

- **Institutional sabotage via appointments and power structures**

The third factor is institutional sabotage – the dismantling of the careful, consultative machinery that used to underpin US trade policymaking.

Nothing illustrates the undermining of an international trade policy process and the side-lining of trade experts better than the 9 April 2025 very public embarrassment of the man who is officially in charge of US trade policy – US Trade Representative Jamieson Greer.

It was supposed to be a routine oversight hearing – part performance, part policy. Jamieson Greer was seated before the House Ways and Means Committee, answering questions about the administration's sweeping new "reciprocal tariffs" announced just a week earlier, on 2 April. Greer, though relatively unknown in public trade circles, was the top official charged with implementing the tariffs. At least, that was the theory.

Greer was literally mid-sentence when President Trump announced, on social media, an enormous climbdown from his historic 2 April tariffs.[12]

How do we know Greer was unaware of this major change in US trade policy? Because it is all on camera. Midway through an exchange with a congressman about cheese quotas, Greer's phone buzzed. He glanced down, then froze. A reporter's camera caught the moment. A push notification lit up his screen:

"BREAKING: Trump announces 90-day suspension of most 'reciprocal tariffs' to allow 'friendly countries' a chance to negotiate fair terms."

Greer blinked, looked to his deputy, then faced the committee. His mic was still hot.

"I... I have not been briefed on that statement," he said. "I'll need to verify whether that's official policy or... a reflection of the President's – uh – position in real time."

This revealed, on camera, just how chaotic the president's trade policy is. How disconnected it is from the machinery that is supposed to guide, develop, and implement it. USTR Greer, nominally one of the most important trade ministers in the world, was reduced to a spectator. He found out this history-shaping policy change in the same way everyone else did, via social media.

To highlight the lack of clear procedures, the day before, on 8 April, Greer had testified to US Senators that: "The president has been clear, again, that he's not doing exemptions or exceptions in the near term".[13]

---

12 PBS NewsHour. (2025, April 9). WATCH: 'This is amateur hour.' Rep. Horsford blasts US trade rep after Trump tariff pause. PBS NewsHour. https://www.pbs.org/newshour/politics/watch-this-is-amateur-hour-rep-horsford-blasts-u-s-trade-rep-after-trump-tariff-pause
13 Erickson, B., & Lawder, D. (2025, April 8). US trade rep faces bipartisan questions on scope and duration of tariffs. Reuters. https://www.reuters.com/world/us/us-trade-rep-faces-bipartisan-questions-scope-duration-tariffs-2025-04-08/

In normal administrations, a shift like Trump's 9 April social media post would follow days of internal debate and interagency discussion. Observers wondering whether US trade policy was supported by any sort of institutionalised process got their answer with the buzz of Greer's phone on the witness stand.

Bulldozing the checks and balances in America's trade policy process

Before 2025, US trade policy was slow and deliberate – a veritable choreography of consultation.

The USTR convened interagency meetings that brought in the view of the Departments of State, Treasury, Commerce, Agriculture, Labor, Defense, and more. Lawyers scrutinised the implications, economists ran impact models, and the voices of industry, unions, and civil society organisations were heard.

I participated in this process when I was following trade matters for the Council of Economic Advisers under President Bush Sr. That was a different era, but the process hadn't changed all that much until January 2025. It wasn't always pretty, and it certainly wasn't fast. But it was robust and predictable. It ensured that America's trade policy served multiple national interests – strategic, economic, political. More to the point, it ensured that the word "chaos" was the last thing that came to mind when the American president talked trade in public.

Trump's appointments sealed the gutting of the traditional interagency process. He did not appoint, for example, a seasoned trade negotiator like Robert Lighthizer, as he did in his first term. He selected a relatively junior trade lawyer with no public profile and no record of independent thought in trade policy – Jaime Greer. Greer's main claim to fame was having been the Chief of Staff of the USTR in Trump's first administration.

The USTR was placed under the tutelage of the Secretary of Commerce, Howard Lutnick. Lutnick is the sort of man that President Trump seems to listen to. He has $3 billion and was a CEO of one of the globalist elite institutions, Cantor Fritzgerald.[14] Lutnick is frequently photographed with the president; Greer less so.

In the trade policy province of Trumpland, as elsewhere, appointees' qualifications seem justified by loyalty rather than expertise. Notably, no prominent trade economists were brought into the administration – effectively eliminating informed debate within the executive branch on the costs, structure, or long-term consequences of US trade strategy.

The result is the chaos we've seen. The sudden imposition of tariffs – without notice, consultation, or clear justification – has systematically cut out the usual players.

14 Diongson, D. (2025, March 16). Howard Lutnick's net worth: From Wall Street heavyweight to Commerce Secretary. TheStreet. https://www.thestreet.com/personalities/howard-lutnick-net-worth

The case for malevolence: Two darker explanations

The arguments in this school of thought can sound like a conspiracy theory, but serious analysts are promoting this view. There are two main points to consider. The first is that the trade chaos is a smokescreen for a presidential power grab. The second is that the tariffs turn US industry leaders into ring-kissers, and thus mute yet another possible source of opposition to the shift towards highly centralised power.

On the first, Levisky and Way wrote an article in Foreign Affairs titled, "The Path to American Authoritarianism."[15] On the second, see for example, US Senator Chris Murphy's recent FT OpEd claiming: "Switching tariffs on and off, and granting exemptions for your political allies, is not about trade policy. It is about bringing American industry to heel."[16]

Trade chaos as camouflage for centralising power

At first glance, Trump's chaotic trade policy might look like simple disorganisation – or the result of a president who just doesn't care to read the fine print. But there's a darker explanation that deserves serious attention: the chaos may be the point.

Unpredictable tariffs. Last-minute reversals. Sudden threats against allies. This isn't just impulsiveness. It's camouflage – a political smokescreen that distracts the public and weakens institutional resistance while power is quietly consolidated in the executive branch. Think of the chaos as a cover for power moves.

In short, the interpretation here is that the chaos is being used – quite deliberately – as a distraction tactic, allowing Trump to reshape the institutional structure of American governance under the radar.

Even more troubling than chaos for its own sake is the possibility that this chaos is being exploited for personal or political gain.

Tariffs as patronage

This strand could be called trade policy as a payoff machine. Indeed, the classic academic article on this is titled: "Protection for Sale".[17] When tariffs are imposed erratically – and exemptions granted just as erratically – it creates the perfect environment for something far more dangerous than bad economics: lobbying, back-handers, or payoffs.

In a properly functioning system, trade policy follows clear rules. Tariffs are debated. Costs and benefits are weighed. Affected sectors are consulted. But under Trump's second administration, tariffs have become so discretionary, so opaque, and so fast-moving that predictability has collapsed – and in the rubble, patronage thrives.

15 Levitsky, S., & Way, L. A. (2025, February 11). The path to American authoritarianism: What comes after democratic breakdown? *Foreign Affairs*. https://www.foreignaffairs.com/united-states/path-american-authoritarianism-trump

16 Murphy, C. (2025, April 17). Trump's tariff policy has nothing to do with trade: The president is using economic warfare to compel corporate loyalty. *Financial Times*, Op-Ed. https://www.ft.com/content/6d0c25e1-f8e5-43d6-88eb-5587df9f58a1

17 Grossman, G. M., & Helpman, E. (1994). Protection for sale. *American Economic Review*, 84(4), 833-850.

Consider what occurred after Trump raised Chinese tariffs to 145%:

- A tariff is announced on Chinese exports of smartphones.

- The next day, Apple's CEO – a known Trump donor – talks to Trump and iPhones receive an exemption from the announced 150% tariff.

The exemption process has become a black box. In that sense, tariff exemptions have become a form of political currency – a way to reward friends, punish critics, and incentivise silence.

It's not always about donations; sometimes it's about public loyalty. CEOs who praise the administration find their industries spared. Those who speak out? They're reminded that their supply chains depend on the goodwill of a very centralised – and very personal – trade apparatus.

More troublingly, it hints at a system where economic levers are repurposed for political control. Trade policy becomes a tool not for national strategy, but for personal power consolidation. This view, which I think is too extreme in its bald form, asserts that the chaos isn't about policy. This is a shakedown wearing a policy mask.

Summary and concluding remarks

Those who lean towards the malevolence theory – which is a bit too conspiracy theory-ish for my tastes – view the chaos as a means to some end that has nothing to do with lifting up the downtrodden middle class, or balancing trade, or reindustrialising America, or national security. It is, they say, part of the smokescreen that hides an unprecedented shift of power to the Oval Office. Or, it is an elegant protection racket where US special interests have to pay in lucre or loyalty to avoid having their business interest cratered by sky-high tariffs.

The incompetence school of thought (which is my current favourite) is more straightforward. The foundation is a bull-headed leader who often declares himself to be the world's greatest thinker on [this space left intentionally blank], and who works in a very closed wishful thinking bubble that his advisors dare not burst. The chaos, in short, is driven by powerful instincts developed in the real estate world and applied unvarnished to running a $26 trillion dollar economy. The instincts are untampered by facts, careful planning, or any sort of economic analysis.

The uncomfortable, yet realistic, answer is that it seems to be a mixture. Incompetency surely plays a big role, and the 'malevolence' argument, while important, might be overstated and slip into conspiracy theory territory.

My problem with conspiracy theories is that they assume a level of coordination and competence that's just not realistic. In my experience, it's hard enough to get five people to agree on which movie to watch. Imagine trying to orchestrate a massive, secret plot.

Nevertheless, there are surely members of the Trump administration who leverage the media misdirection to advance their causes.

From the incompetence perspective, three distinct factors fuel the chaos, in my view.

- First, Trump's personal business experience, which is grounded in 1970s real estate bargaining, favours unpredictability and brinkmanship as a deliberate negotiation strategy. This instinctive approach, honed through years in the rough-and-tumble world of New York real estate, is surely one of the most important sources of the chaos we've all wondered about. Moreover, he was running a family business and is now applying those management lessons to a 170 million-strong workforce.

- Second, Trump's reality TV experience conditions him to view tariffs as theatrical performances designed to project strength when implemented and wisdom when reversed. The spectacle itself – rapid impositions followed by partial retreats – becomes the primary goal, overshadowing economic rationale and causing damaging uncertainty.

- Third, institutional sabotage has systematically dismantled the careful interagency process historically responsible for US trade policy. By subordinating USTR under Commerce and filling key positions with inexperienced loyalists, Trump ensures that decisions reflect personal whims rather than national strategic interests.

On the dark side, I would say there is some evidence supporting the hypothesis of malevolence.

Tariffs seem to be, increasingly, instruments of patronage and political coercion. They reward business leaders and donors who publicly express loyalty while punishing critics through selective exemptions. This creates a form of corruption where economic policy is dangerously intertwined with personal and political loyalty. At some level, this is just lobbying, but I think what we are seeing in Washington is beyond the norm.

The malevolence is, probably, not premeditated. Trump's chaotic tariff policy likely originated in instinct-driven incompetence, but has been weaponised by political operatives around him who recognised chaos as an opportunity for authoritarian-style centralisation.

Closing remarks

The broader consequences of normalising chaos in trade policy are already undermining the administration's own goal of repatriating manufacturing. This requires long-term investment, which, in turn, requires predictability. And yet, this administration is governing as if predictability were a weakness.

Theatrics may achieve short-term political gains, but the long-term costs are mounting. Supply chains are disrupted. Investment is suppressed. America's trading partners are disoriented.

Most dangerously, America and the world risk growing numb to it all. When chaos becomes the norm, we stop noticing its corrosive effects on trust, governance, and the economy. Allies lose confidence. Businesses delay decisions. The soft power the US painstakingly built over decades erodes.

In the end, Trump's tariff policy is neither a blunder nor a blueprint. It is, in my view, a collision of instinctive incompetence and opportunistic control.

The chaos isn't just a feature or a bug. It's a red warning light on the dashboard of American democracy.

4   Why tariffs won't help the middle class but still win in Washington
Politics replaces real economic medicine with tariff placebos

When President Trump was first elected, markets rallied. Despite his loud protectionist campaign rhetoric, investors seemed to assume it was just talk. Tariffs, they believed, were bluster for the base, not a blueprint for governance. Stock prices surged in anticipation of deregulation, tax cuts, and business-friendly policymaking. Here's a typical quote from the time:

> *"Trump crying wolf over tariffs has already convinced Wall Street that threats will be short-lived."*
>
> *– Eleanor Pringle, Fortune, 4 February 2025*

Turns out, he wasn't crying wolf. He brought the wolf and loosed it on the trading system.

Markets realised this when the president launched his Great Trade Hack on 2 April. Financial markets reeled. Bond prices dropped. The dollar spiked, stocks slid, and economists issued dire forecasts.

But by mid May, markets were back to pre-2 April levels. It seems that many believe America is going back to normal.

They are wrong. This chapter explains why protectionism is here to stay, why tariffs cannot help the American middle class, and why – despite their economic ineffectiveness – they remain political winners. US protectionism isn't here because tariffs work economically – they don't. It's mainstream since it performs politically.

The chapter begins by showing that US protectionist tendencies are far from new. The forces started building just after the Global Financial Crisis and the Great Recession that followed.

The chapter then turns to the key economic point – one of the most important of the whole book. Tariffs cannot help the middle class. I'm not saying "probably won't"; I'm saying "can't." At best, tariffs can only help Americans with jobs in goods-producing sectors, but less than one in ten members of the middle class have such jobs.

The chapter then ties the points together to conclude that is shocking but also obvious once you focus on three facts:

1. Tariffs don't work economically.

2. The policies that would work are politically toxic since they require higher taxes and bigger government.

3. Tariffs work politically as placebos for the malaise. Protectionism fills the policy vacuum with theatrical gestures.

This is a self-reinforcing loop: the middle-class crisis fuels protectionism, protectionism fails to solve the crisis, and that failure deepens the demand for performative tariffs.

The upshot is clear. Tariffs are here to stay. Not because they work, but because they perform.

We all have to get used to a protectionist America.

The post-2008 collapse of the trade consensus

To understand why US protectionism is here to stay, we have to step back and see where it came from. The story doesn't start with Trump. It starts with a bipartisan consensus that broke down quietly after the 2008 Global Financial Crisis.

From the 1980s through the early 2000s, US trade policy was marked by a pro-trade consensus. From Ronald Reagan through George W. Bush, trade policy was so consistent and so bipartisan that it was almost boring.

Differences of degree existed, but Washington's political compass always pointed to support for open, rules-based trade and support for the world trade system that supported it. Both parties saw trade as a tool of prosperity, diplomacy, and global influence.

For instance, Reagan launched the Uruguay Round and the Canada–US Free Trade Agreement. Bush Sr. expanded that to NAFTA and opened talks for dozens more free trade agreements with partners around the world. Clinton continued the tradition by spending abundant political capital on transforming the loose-knit General Agreement on Tariffs and Trade (GATT) into an official institution: the World Trade Organisation (WTO).

Bush Jr. leaned into the pro-trade consensus by doing 11 free trade agreements (the most of any post-war president). And he championed China's entry into the WTO.

Then came the crash – the Global Financial Crisis of 2008-2009.

The Crisis heightened middle-class resentment is two ways. First, the recession, painful and prolonged as it was, hit middle-class livelihoods hard. Second, it reinforced middle-class views that the system was rigged against them.

While US workers suffered, US banks got bailed out. Worst yet, none of the bankers who caused the pain went to jail.

Washington reacted by reaching for trade as a scapegoat. Trade, in Washington, became a four-lettered word. Barack Obama didn't campaign on protectionism, but his administration put every trade deal on hold. The ongoing multilateral trade talks, known as the Doha Round, were stripped of the US support they would have needed to come to a successful conclusion. Obama had his trade representative put an end the Round in 2012.

While America wasn't protectionist at this point, the US was doing no bilateral, multilateral, or unilateral trade liberalisation. Think of it as trade hesitancy.

Donald Trump's 2016 election turned the hesitancy into hostility. His administration was openly and vocally anti-free trade. He talked about trade as a zero-sum struggle. For the first time in the modern era, the US president was campaigning against trade liberalisation. The Republican Party – the historic home of free trade – transformed itself into a vehicle for protectionism dressed in economic nationalism.

But what's equally revealing is what happened next. When Joe Biden took office in 2021, he didn't reverse Trump's tariffs; he kept nearly all of them in place. He spoke of rebuilding alliances, but also of "Buy American". The tone softened, but the trajectory remained. This was polite protectionism, but it was still protectionism.

By the time Trump returned to office in 2025, the bipartisan road to protectionism was already paved. In this sense, his "Great Trade Hack" was a continuation, not an aberration.

Here's how the trajectory looks over time:

Years	US trade policy
1981-1993	Reagan to Bush Sr: *Super pro-trade*
1994-2008	Clinton to Bush Jr: *Super pro-trade*
2009-2016	Obama I & II: *Trade hesitancy*
2017-2020	Trump I: *Trade hostility*
2021-2024	Biden: *Trade hesitancy*
2025-2029	Trump II: *Trade hostility unbound*

Why tariffs can't help the middle class

At the heart of US trade policy today lies a contradiction. President Trump presents tariffs as the miracle cure for middle-class hardship. But tariffs can't do that because they don't touch the parts of the economy where most of the middle class works.

The truth is that middle-class Americans are not factory workers. They are nurses, teachers, office administrators, retail managers, IT professionals, and restaurant workers. The share of middle-class employment in manufacturing – often used as the political poster child for tariffs – is now below 9%. Add agriculture and mining, and the tradable goods sector still employs fewer than one in ten middle-class workers.

Let's look at the numbers. In 2022, middle-class households were defined by Pew as earning between roughly $60,000 and $180,000 for a family of three. These workers are spread across a wide range of sectors, but are overwhelmingly concentrated in service-producing, not goods-producing, sectors. Here are the facts:

MIDDLE-CLASS EMPLOYMENT IN THE US BY SECTOR, 2022

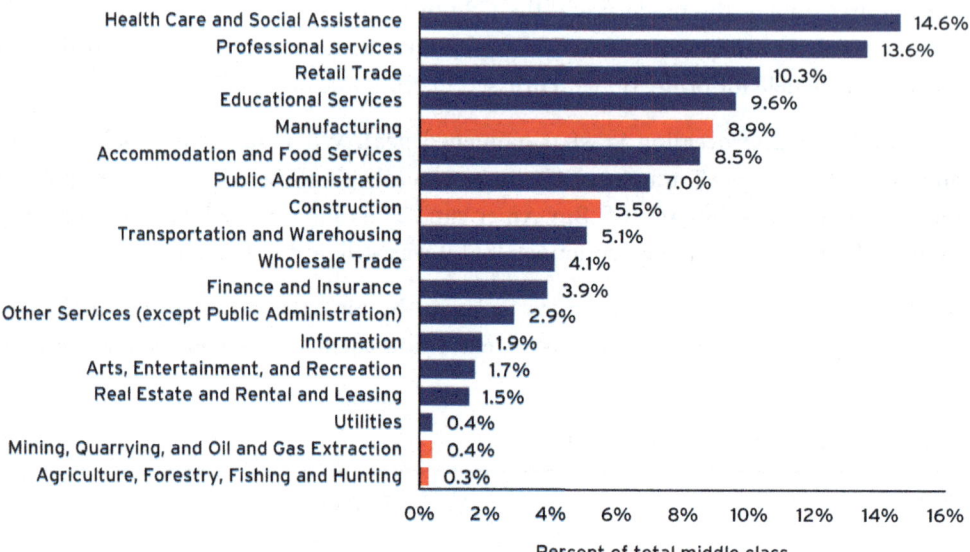

Source: Author's calculations based on US employment by sector and Pew Research middle class employment data[1] Data available on request.

The largest single middle-class employment sector is healthcare and social assistance, at 18.5%. These are nurses, technicians, therapists, home health aides. Next comes professional services (15.3%), which includes engineers, consultants, lawyers, and managers. Then retail (11.7%), education (10.1%), and leisure and hospitality (9.4%). These five sectors alone account for nearly two-thirds of middle-class employment.

As noted above, manufacturing accounts for just 9%. Agriculture and mining combined? Less than 1%.

Even if tariffs were perfectly designed to protect domestic industry, they could, at best, directly assist only about one in ten middle-class workers.

1   Calculations based on US employment by sector (US Bureau of Labor Statistics. (2023). Occupational Employment Statistics: All data, May 2023 (OESM23ALL). US Department of Labor. https://www.bls.gov/oes/special-requests/oesm23all.zip) and Pew Research middle-class employment data (Kochhar, R. (2024, May 31). The state of the American middle class. Pew Research Center. https://www.pewresearch.org/race-and-ethnicity/2024/05/31/the-state-of-the-american-middle-class/)

The other nine out of ten will only see tariff-induced price increases that will lower their purchasing power. On net, the tariffs will probably harm the middle class.

That's the first fatal flaw: few middle-class workers have jobs in the sectors that protectionism protects.

The second is mechanical: it is not possible to put tariffs on services. A tariff is applied at a border, on goods crossing into a country. But services don't cross borders in the same way. A haircut, a hospital visit, a childcare shift, a classroom hour – these aren't imported. They happen locally. Even in traded services like finance and consulting, the US enjoys a comparative advantage and runs a surplus.

Moreover, most services simply aren't tradable, so there are no imports to tariff – even if you wanted to. For most service-sector workers, there is no foreign competition to protect against.

More fundamentally, tariffs don't address the root causes of middle-class malaise. The US middle class isn't falling behind because of cheap imports. It's falling behind because of decades of underinvestment in the policies that create economic security: universal healthcare, affordable education, labour power, progressive taxation, and housing affordability.

Other countries have managed to support their middle classes not by walling off trade, but by cushioning its impacts. Canada, Germany, the Nordics – these economics are also open to trade. But they've built robust systems of redistribution, social insurance, and public goods that absorb economic shocks. They don't fear globalisation because they've equipped their people to survive it.

The US has chosen a different path. It relies on markets to deliver fairness and security – and when they don't, it reaches for symbols instead of solutions. Tariffs are one such symbol. They allow politicians to claim they're defending the middle class, while avoiding the policies that would actually help but carry political cost.

In short: tariffs cannot help the middle class. They are structurally misaligned with how the US economy works. They target the wrong sectors, fail to touch the real sources of distress, and often backfire on consumers.

But – and this is the political core of protectionism's popularity in Washington – they make politicians look like they care. Tariffs have become the reusable placebo of American economic policy.

Conclusion: Why tariffs will persist

Tariffs don't help the middle class. That's the economic reality. They fail to reach the sectors where most middle-class Americans work since they can't be applied to services. They don't fix the structural problems driving middle-class malaise – wage stagnation, insecure employment, unaffordable healthcare, education, and housing. In fact, by raising prices on everyday goods, they make life harder for the very people they claim to protect.

And yet, tariffs are politically triumphant. They survive changes in leadership. They cross party lines. They are not an aberration of the Trump years. They are now a bipartisan habit. A default setting.

Why? Because while they fail economically, they succeed emotionally and politically. They are the ideal symbolic substitute – simple, aggressive, reassuring. Patriotic even. They provide the illusion of protection without the cost of real structural change.

They let politicians say, "We're doing something", while avoiding policies that break political taboos, namely, a stronger social policy that would require bigger government and higher taxes.

This is the looping GIF of American protectionism:

- Middle-class malaise creates pressure to act.

- Real solutions are politically toxic.

- Politicians reach for protection to divert blame.

- Protection fails to help, so the malaise persists.

- That persistence feeds the next round of performative protectionism.

This, I believe, is how the US went from free trader to protectionist.

The lesson of this chapter is simple and stark. America's trade war didn't begin with Trump, and it certainly won't end with him. Protectionism is America's new normal.

Ironically, US tariffs will persist not <u>despite</u> their economic ineffectiveness, but because of it.

5 Why is Trump's trade policy so chaotic?

Why protectionism won't rebuild American industry

"April 2, 2025, will forever be remembered as the day American industry was reborn, the day America's destiny was reclaimed, and the day that we began to make America wealthy again."

– President Donald J. Trump.[1]

With these words, President Trump promised nothing less than a second industrial revolution, made in America and made by tariffs. His message was clear: bring back factories, restore blue-collar pride, and rebuild the economic might of the United States by taxing foreign imports.

It's hard to argue with this goal. America does need a stronger, more resilient manufacturing base – if nothing else to ensure it can produce the military equipment it needs to defend itself.

The key message of this chapter is that the Great Trade Hack won't achieve the goal. That's a judgement about means, not goals. There is, in fact, a strong case for rebuilding parts of America's manufacturing base.

The case for judicious reindustrialisation

From the 1970s, America – like all rich nations – underwent a structural shift from factory work to services, driven by automation and globalisation.[2] But unlike Japan, Germany, France and others, the US dismantled its industrial policy. That left the free market to guide which manufacturing sectors were downsized and by how much.[3,4] This "hands-off" approach, rooted in Reagan-era market fundamentalism, starved the state of funds and legitimacy it would have needed to guide American manufacturing.[5]

In the warm glow of the post-Cold War world, that stance may have been defensible, but now it looks reckless. Trade and supply chains are being weaponised by nations

1   Hutzler, A. (2025, April 3). Trump rolls out sweeping tariffs as he deems deficits a 'national emergency'. ABC News. Retrieved May 1, 2025, from https://abcnews.go.com/Politics/trumps-liberation-day-arrives-gambles-big-risky-tariff/story?id=120382209
2   Baldwin, R. (2019, November 7). Globalisation, automation and the history of work: Looking back to understand the future. UNCTAD. Retrieved May 1, 2025, from https://unctad.org/news/globalisation-automation-and-history-work-looking-back-understand-future
3   US Congress, Office of Technology Assessment. (1981). US industrial competitiveness: A comparison of steel, electronics, and automobiles (OTA-ITE-198). Washington, DC: US Government Printing Office. Retrieved from https://www.princeton.edu/~ota/disk3/1981/8133/813314.PDF
4   Rodrik, D. (2022, September). An industrial policy for good jobs (Policy Proposal). The Hamilton Project, Brookings Institution. https://drodrik.scholar.harvard.edu/files/dani-rodrik/files/rodrik_-_an_industrial_policy_for_good_jobs.pdf
5   Wade, R. H. (2014). The paradox of US industrial policy: The developmental state in disguise. In Transforming economies: Making industrial policy work for growth, jobs and development (pp. 379-400). International Labour Organization. https://www.ilo.org/sites/default/files/wcmsp5/groups/public/@dgreports/@inst/documents/publication/wcms_315679.pdf

including the US.[6,7] Covid exposed supply chain fragilities.[8,9] Key US capabilities – like 5G, semiconductors, and shipbuilding – were lost not by design, but by drift.

Right goal, wrong policy

So let me be very clear: reindustrialisation is necessary. But Trump's tariffs won't do the trick.

This chapter is not a "don't do it" argument – it's a "don't do it this way" argument.

Tariffs cannot reverse decades of economic transformation on their own. They can't rebuild capabilities, foster innovation, or coordinate investment. Often, they backfire – raising costs for downstream industries and hurting the very workers they claim to protect.

In the pages ahead, I'll explain why tariffs are the wrong tool, look at why US manufacturing weakened in the first place, and explore what a modern industrial policy could look like. Not a nostalgic return to the 1950s, but a forward-looking strategy for building the industries of the 2050s.

Because if the US wants to make things again, it needs to start by making smart policy.

Why reindustrialisation matters now

Reindustrialisation is now a question of national security and technological autonomy.[10,11,12,13] America, and every other rich nation in the world, shifted to a post-industrial society from the 1970s, when industrial automation started automating away the jobs.

The shift from factories to offices was a structural transformation that was less traumatic than the shift from farm to factory, but it reweaved the social, economic, and political fabrics of all the advanced economies. A key element of this was the rise of middle-class malaise discussed in Chapter 2.

6   Feldhaus, L., Huang, Y., Kim, S., Kim, W., Lee, J. S., Marechal, D., Sun, X., & Weiss, S. (2020). The weaponization of trade: A study of modern trade conflicts from the mid-1900s to present (Capstone Report, Spring 2020). Columbia University, School of International and Public Affairs. https://www.sipa.columbia.edu/sites/default/files/migrated/downloads/Capstone%2520Report%2520%2528Eurasia%2520Group%2529.pdf

7   Krantz, T. (2025, April 2). The new geopolitical tensions jeopardizing the global economy. SupplyChainBrain. https://www.supplychainbrain.com/blogs/1-think-tank/post/41369-the-new-geopolitical-tensions-jeopardizing-the-global-economy

8   McGillivray, G. (2024, September 10). An expert explains: What COVID did to global supply chains. World Economic Forum. https://www.weforum.org/stories/2021/07/covid-19-pandemic-global-supply-chains/

9   US Congress Joint Economic Committee. (n.d.). Decades of manufacturing decline and outsourcing left US supply chains vulnerable to disruption [PDF]. Retrieved from https://www.jec.senate.gov/public/_cache/files/94bf8985-1e87-438b-9a3a-e3334489dd30/background-on-issues-in-us-manufacturing-and-supply-chains-final.pdf

10   Bishop, A., & Seitz, B. (2025, February 16). Reindustrialise: Building capacity, security, and prosperity in a de-globalising world. Alliance for Responsible Citizenship. https://www.arcforum.com/research-papers/choices-reindustrialise

11   Biden-Harris Administration. (2025). Building resilience through a Made in America industrial strategy [PDF]. The White House. https://bidenwhitehouse.archives.gov/wp-content/uploads/2025/01/Building-Resilience-through-a-Made-in-America-Industrial-Strategy.final_.pdf

12   RBA Advisors. (2024, March 20). US industrial renaissance: It's a matter of national security. https://www.rbadvisors.com/insights/us-industrial-renaissance-its-a-matter-of-national-security

13   Schadlow, N. (2025). Reindustrialization: A strategy for American sovereignty and security. Hudson Institute. https://www.hudson.org/national-security-defense/reindustrialization-strategy-american-sovereignty-security-nadia-schadlow

America's industrial base became collateral damage in a decades-long experiment with low-tax, small-government, market fundamentalism. That experiment, which began with Ronald Reagan and was carried forward by both parties, starved the public sector of the resources and legitimacy it needed to run a real industrial policy.[14,15]

For years, the idea that government should play an active role in shaping manufacturing was treated as heresy. The Overton Window moved so far to the right that simply acknowledging a role for the state in economic planning could get you shunned. Economists self-censored.

Whether this hands-off stance made sense in the 1990s and early 2000s is open to debate. But what's not debatable is that the world has changed dramatically since then.

America awoke from its "End of History" dream – the comforting idea that an open, rules-based global economy would guide all nations toward liberal democracy, individual rights, and market capitalism. The dream turned out to be just that: a dream.

China, far from becoming a cuddly panda, emerged as a full-spectrum competitor – economic, technological, and military – with a state-led form of capitalism that made it the world's sole manufacturing superpower. Russia, once welcomed into the G8 as a partner, reverted to military aggression. Globalisation, once a symbol of peace through commerce, became a vector for vulnerability. Trade was weaponised. Semiconductors were hoarded. Covid taught us just how fragile global supply chains really were.

In this new world, there are many holes in US industrial capacity that look less like efficiency and more like strategic shortsightedness.

The US cannot manufacture leading-edge semiconductors essential to its most advanced weapons, any of its own 5G telecom infrastructure, large oceangoing ships, including military vessels, or the precursors for many critical pharmaceuticals.

But to be clear, these weren't conscious choices. These vulnerabilities were the product of drift – a naïve faith that global markets would always deliver resilience, security, and fairness. That faith conveniently supported the low-tax, small-government worldview that Republicans embraced since WWII and Democrats embraced since Bill Clinton was president.

14   Baker, D. (1998). The public investment deficit: Two decades of neglect threaten 21st century economy (Briefing Paper). Economic Policy Institute. https://www.epi.org/publication/briefingpapers_pubinv/
15   Calidas, D., & Li, C. (2025, March 10). Beyond rhetoric: The enduring political appeal of US industrial policy for critical and strategic technologies. Belfer Center for Science and International Affairs, Harvard Kennedy School. Retrieved May 1, 2025, from https://www.belfercenter.org/research-analysis/beyond-rhetoric-us-industrial-policy

Why US manufacturing weakened

"President Donald J. Trump is standing up for American workers, strengthening American industries, and making clear to the world that America will no longer be ripped off."

The White House, 5 March 2025[16]

A core pillar of President Trump's trade policy is driven by the notion that America has been "ripped off" by the rest of the world – that unfair trade practices abroad explain the hollowing out of US manufacturing.

This line of thinking underpins the case for tariffs: if foreign competitors played dirty to steal America's factories, the solution is to hit back hard and bring the jobs home.

The facts tell a different story

From the 1990s, the world witnessed an epic shift. Manufacturing relocated from the world's richest economies to a handful of emerging ones. The G7 dominated global manufacturing until the late 1990s, accounting for nearly two-thirds of global industrial output. But by the mid-2000s, this dominance began to slip. The G7's collective share of world manufacturing fell – and almost every percentage point they lost was picked up by a group of six emerging economies: China, India, Korea, Indonesia, Thailand, and Brazil.

These six – call them the "I6" – saw their share of global manufacturing rise nearly one-for-one with the G7's decline. China's rise was especially dramatic. In 1990, it accounted for roughly 3% of world manufacturing; by 2020, it held over 20%.

WORLD MANUFACTURING SHARES: G7, I6 AND THE REST OF THE WORLD

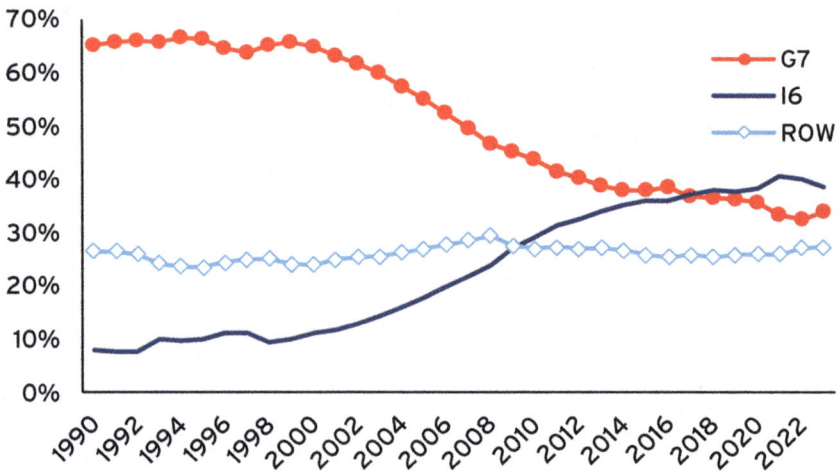

Source: UNIDO National Accounts Database[17]

16 The White House. (2025, March 5). President Trump is putting American workers first - and bringing back American manufacturing. https://www.whitehouse.gov/articles/2025/03/president-trump-is-putting-american-workers-first-and-bringing-back-american-manufacturing/
17 United Nations Industrial Development Organization. (2024). National Accounts Database [Data set]. UNIDO Statistics Portal. https://stat.unido.org/data/download?dataset=national-accounts

So, what explains this tectonic shift? Was it the result of predatory foreign policies? A conspiracy to steal American industry? No, it was not – or at least not mostly.

As I've argued since 2006[18] and explained in depth in *The Great Convergence*,[19] the change began with the ICT revolution of the 1990s. Advances in information and communication technology made it feasible – indeed, profitable – for firms in the G7 to unbundle their production and relocate labour-intensive stages to low-wage economies. This wasn't a new idea (textiles had long done it), but ICT made it work for much more complex products.

With advanced ICT, Canadian aircraft maker Bombardier could now produce the tails of its business jets in central Mexico, secure in the knowledge that they'd fit perfectly onto planes assembled in Quebec. In short, it became possible to run a global supply chain with the same precision you'd once have expected only within a single factory.

And once such things became feasible, the enormous wage gaps between rich and poor countries made it irresistible. The offshoring boom started to boom. Jobs and production were sent by G7 firms to emerging economies.

Here's the critical twist. G7 firms didn't just move production; they moved technology. They brought their know-how and process sophistication to emerging markets. That – more than anything else – was the game-changer.

Suddenly, these emerging economies countries weren't just competing with cheap labour and low-tech goods. They were producing high-quality, technologically advanced components for global supply chains. In the old world, it was high-tech, high-wage versus low-tech, low-wage – and the G7 won. In the new world, it was high-tech, low-wage versus high-tech, high-wage – and that tilted the playing field.

This was not industrial theft. It was a business decision by American firms, and firms based in other G7 nations. It was G7 multinationals, including America's biggest manufacturers, that orchestrated this global relocation of industry. Emerging economies like China, India, and Korea played a role, of course. They created the right conditions – roads, ports, rule of law, basic infrastructure. But they didn't steal industry. They were chosen by the firms that used to make everything in the US, Japan, and Germany.

This explains another striking pattern. Outside the I6, very few developing countries saw major gains in manufacturing – even though many adopted the market-friendly policies known as the "Washington Consensus". In other words, being open and business-friendly wasn't enough. What mattered most was whether G7 firms brought production to you.

18 Baldwin, R. (2006). Globalisation: The great unbundling(s). Secretariat of the Economic Council, Prime Minister's Office, Finland. https://repository.graduateinstitute.ch/record/295612/files/Baldwin_06-09-20.pdf

19 Baldwin, R. (2016). The great convergence: Information technology and the new globalization. The Belknap Press of Harvard University Press.

So, who's to blame for America's industrial decline? Not foreigners. Not China. Not some clever trick by developing countries. The main actors in this shift – at least in its early start-up phase – were firms from America, Japan, Germany, and so on making profit-maximising decisions in response to the new possibilities. ICT made it possible for them to arbitrage massive global wage gaps directly, by moving labour-intensive stages of production to China and other emerging economies.

Trump's tariffs, by contrast, aim at punishing foreign exporters for a transformation that was largely driven by decisions made in corporate boardrooms in Chicago, Cleveland, and Cupertino.

If you want to understand why reindustrialisation is hard, this is where to start. Not with the myth of foreign villains, but with the real structural forces that changed the face of global manufacturing. Offshoring the was the main culprit, not foreigners.[20, 21]

After a while, especially in China, the initial offshoring triggered an industrialisation take-off like the world has never seen. As a consequence, these I6 emerging economies have self-sustaining industrial bases. In particular, China has more than one-third of world gross production of manufacturing, and that agglomeration edge makes it difficult for firms based in other countries to compete on that level. In this sense, offshoring was the spark that triggered industrial take-offs in emerging economies, and thus ultimately a key cause.

In short, if you want to blame somebody for the movement of manufacturing out of the US and to emerging economies, the culprit is American manufacturing companies and their offshoring.

I provide a much more detailed analysis of this offshoring deindustrialisation driven by offshoring in my 2016 book, *The Great Convergence*, if you want to see more detailed evidence.

Strategic holes: The industrial gaps that tariffs can't fill

America didn't just lose manufacturing jobs over the past few decades – it lost critical capabilities. As global supply chains stretched and domestic production shrank, key gaps quietly opened in the US industrial base. These are no longer abstract concerns. They are strategic liabilities in a world where trade is being weaponised (with the US being a leader in this). In addition to the geopolitical shocks, international supply chains have become more fragile due to the climate change-driven rise in severe weather events, financial crises, and pandemics.

20 Broecke, S. (2024). Offshoring, reshoring, and the evolving geography of jobs: A scoping paper (OECD Social, Employment and Migration Working Papers No. 308). Organisation for Economic Co-operation and Development. https://dx.doi.org/10.1787/adc9a9d5-en

21 Coulter, S., Kakkad, J., & Britto, D. (2021). Home advantage? Rhetoric versus reality in the reshoring debate. Tony Blair Institute for Global Change. https://institute.global/insights/economic-prosperity/home-advantage-rhetoric-versus-reality-reshoring-debate

While other advanced economies have similar problems, many of them avoided the worst by maintaining strategically focused industrial policies. US peers like France, Japan, and Germany – to say nothing of Korea and China – paid attention to their strategic capabilities.[22,23,24] The result is that the US is particularly exposed to the recent shift to a more dangerous, less cooperative global economy.

Top of the list: leading-edge semiconductors. The chips that power America's most advanced weapons systems – stealth fighters, missile guidance, secure communications – are made abroad, mostly in Taiwan. Not even one US firm can fabricate chips at the technological frontier. That's not just a supply chain problem. It's a national security vulnerability.[25]

Then there's shipbuilding. The United States, a global naval power, can no longer build large oceangoing commercial vessels. Even military shipbuilding has become dangerously reliant on foreign components, shrinking yards, and ageing workforces. Should conflict arise, ramping up maritime capacity would be slow and painful – if it's even possible.[26,27]

And on the economic security front, the picture is no better. The US depends heavily on foreign sources for pharmaceutical precursors, generic drugs, and medical equipment.[28,29] Covid-19 didn't create these vulnerabilities, it revealed them. Basic personal protective equipment (PPE) was scarce. Antibiotic supplies ran low. Americans learned the hard way that "just in time" can quickly become "not in time."

The list goes on. Rare earth elements? Mined and refined mostly in China. Solar panels and batteries? Designed in the US, but manufactured elsewhere. Even 5G telecom gear, which forms the backbone of the modern economy, is almost entirely made abroad – mostly in countries the US doesn't fully trust.

These gaps weren't created by one bad trade deal or one tariff cut. They were the unintended consequences of drift – of assuming that market forces alone would

22 Ruta, M., & Jakubik, A. (2024, October 29). The renaissance of industrial policy: Known knowns, known unknowns, and unknown unknowns. World Bank Blogs. https://blogs.worldbank.org/en/developmenttalk/the-renaissance-of-industrial-policy--known-knowns--known-unknow

23 Bruegel. (2023). Cooperation or conflict? Will industrial policy produce more winners than losers? In Bruegel Blueprint 33, Chapter 5. https://www.bruegel.org/sites/default/files/2023-07/Bruegel%20Blueprint%2033_chapter%205.pdf

24 Durdu, J. (2025, April 2). The strategic importance of China-Japan-South Korea collaboration. CGTN. https://news.cgtn.com/news/2025-04-02/The-strategic-importance-of-China-Japan-South-Korea-collaboration-1Cfa7gemMLK/p.html

25 Shivakumar, S., & Wessner, C. W. (2022, August 8). Semiconductors and national defense: What are the stakes? Center for Strategic and International Studies. https://www.csis.org/analysis/semiconductors-and-national-defense-what-are-stakes

26 Weddle, B., Mellors, N., Brukardt, R., Voelker, A., Plum, B., & Cassady, S. (2024, June 5). Charting a new course: The untapped potential of American shipyards. McKinsey & Company. https://www.mckinsey.com/industries/aerospace-and-defense/our-insights/charting-a-new-course-the-untapped-potential-of-american-shipyards

27 Thompson, L. (2024, February 8). The US commercial ship industry has collapsed. Fallout for national security could follow. Forbes. https://www.forbes.com/sites/lorenthompson/2024/02/08/the-us-commercial-ship-industry-has-collapsed-fallout-for-national-security-could-follow/

28 Schondelmeyer, S. W. (2024, February 6). A resilient US drug supply: Current & emerging vulnerabilities [Testimony before the US House Committee on Ways & Means]. https://democrats-waysandmeans.house.gov/sites/evo-subsites/democrats-waysandmeans.house.gov/files/evo-media-document/!Schondelmeyer%20Testimony%20House%20Ways%20%20Means%20Shortages%202024-02-06%20v2.pdf

29 Bown, C. P., & Bollyky, T. J. (2020, April 8). The US reliance on other countries for essential medical equipment. VoxEU (CEPR Policy Portal). https://cepr.org/voxeu/columns/us-reliance-other-countries-essential-medical-equipment

maintain resilience and readiness. They didn't. And now, plugging these holes will take more than import taxes. It will take seriously sustained industrial strategy.

Why America let its guard down

For decades after the Cold War, America lived in what might be called the "End of History dream." The phrase, coined by political scientist Francis Fukuyama, captured a powerful idea: that the grand ideological battles of the 20th century were over. Market-led democracy had triumphed. Communism had collapsed. The future would be open, rules-based, and peaceful.

At first, the world seemed to validate this optimism. Russia was invited to join the G7, transforming it into the G8. China, India, and much of the emerging world embraced open trade, welcomed foreign investment, and appeared to be converging with Western norms. For a while, China looked like a cuddly panda. The West hoped that rising incomes would eventually bring political liberalisation.

But the panda turned out to be a dragon. China grew more authoritarian at home and assertive abroad. Xi Jinping made himself president for life and began aggressively pressing territorial claims in the South China Sea. China's industrial policy was an historic success, leading it to become the world's sole manufacturing superpower. An asymmetric supply-chain dependence arose whereby all nations in the world became more reliant on Chinese industrial inputs than vice versa. Russia reverted to Soviet form and invaded Ukraine, first in Crimea and the east. In 2022, these incursions turned into a full-blown invasion aimed at taking over the whole country by force. Once that happened, it was clear that the End of History dream was an illusion.

All this might have remained abstract had Covid not woken the world up. Suddenly, the comforting dream of frictionless global supply chains gave way to the reality of fragility. Medical gear, pharmaceuticals, semiconductors – many turned out to be sourced almost entirely from abroad, including from rivals like China.

The United States, lulled by the End of History narrative, had let its industrial guard down. In the spirit of cost-cutting and market fundamentalism, both Democratic and Republican administrations accepted the idea that economic security could be left to the private sector. Even military contractors got in on the act – offshoring components, including to China, the very country that is now viewed as America's chief strategic competitor.[30] What began as dreamland has become a cautionary tale. Economic and national security cannot be left to the private sector alone.

30 Michienzi, C. (2025, March 12). Finding adversaries hiding in the Defense Department's supply chains. War on the Rocks. https://warontherocks.com/2025/03/finding-adversaries-hiding-in-the-defense-departments-supply-chains/

Did all the manufacturing jobs go to China?

Let's start with a surprising fact. Since 2013, the world has lost about 20 million manufacturing jobs.[31] That's not a typo. The global manufacturing workforce is shrinking – even though global manufacturing output has kept growing.

What's going on here? A common suspicion – one that is held firmly by the Trump administration – is that these jobs were "stolen" by China and others. But the data say otherwise. Ironically, it was China who was the biggest loser of jobs by far. Between 2013 and 2018, China alone shed 22.8 million factory jobs – more than the world's net decline.[32] In other words, if you're looking for where the jobs went, China isn't the destination.

This is a sign of something deeper and really important to understand when thinking about reindustrialising America. China is becoming a normal mega-economy. Its industrial productivity is rising. And today, just like what happened in the US or Germany in earlier decades, higher productivity means fewer Chinese workers are needed to make more stuff. Globalisation and offshoring were the main cause of US factory job losses. Automation was the culprit.

What about the G7 nations?

Victimisation plays a star role in President Trump's view of why so many Americans are suffering in the midst of plenty. Chapter 2 argued that globalisation was not the cause of middle-class malaise in the US; instead it was the globalisation and technology shocks in the absence of well-functioning social and adjustment policies.

To stress this in the context of deindustrialisation and job loss, it is important to start with how widespread this rich-nation deindustrialisation is. The US is the only G7 nation to run massive and decades-long trade deficits, but every G7 nation experienced a similar loss of world manufacturing market share.[33,34] It was only the US that had the "burden" of a reserve currency, but its manufacturing shock was shared by other G7 nations that do not have a reserve currency.

The story for the G7 is more nuanced than it is at the world level. From 1995 to 2010, the G7 lost about 13 million manufacturing jobs. But since 2010, they've actually gained

31 Handley, K. (2024). What happened to US manufacturing? The evidence on technology, trade, and structural change (Technical Analysis Working Paper No. 2024-07). Economic Innovation Group. https://eig.org/wp-content/uploads/2024/07/TAWP-Handley.pdf

32 Organisation for Economic Co-operation and Development. (2023). Trade in employment (TiM) [Data set]. OECD Data Explorer.
https://data-explorer.oecd.org/vis?lc=en&tm=Trade%20in%20employment&pg=0&snb=163&df[ds]=dsDisseminateFinalDMZ&df[id]=DSD_TIM_2023%40DF_TIM_2023&df[ag]=OECD.STI.PIE&df[vs]=1.0&dq=EMPN.CHN.C%2B_T.W..A&pd=1995%2C2020&to[TIME_PERIOD]=false&vw=tb

33 Council on Foreign Relations. (2025, April 23). The US trade deficit: How much does it matter? https://www.cfr.org/backgrounder/us-trade-deficit-how-much-does-it-matter

34 Trading Economics. (2025, April 3). United States balance of trade. https://tradingeconomics.com/united-states/balance-of-trade

around 2 million. Their share of global manufacturing jobs, which had plummeted from 20% in 1995 to 13% by 2013, has inched back up slightly.[35]

India, often seen as a rising manufacturing giant, followed a different arc. It added 13 million jobs between 1995 and 2010, then lost 6 million between 2010 and 2018.[36] So no, the jobs didn't all go to India either.

The rest of the world? That's where things get interesting. Emerging markets outside China and India gained about 7 million factory jobs since 2010. That makes them, along with the G7, the relative winners in the post-2010 job reshuffle.

So where did the jobs go?

They didn't go anywhere. They disappeared. They were automated away.

This is Economics 101. Employment depends on two things: first, the total amount of work to be done; and second, how much work each employee can do per hour – productivity. At the global level, the "offshoring" explanation doesn't work. There's no "overseas" for the planet. If global factory employment shrinks while output keeps rising, the reason is simple – rising productivity.

That's what happened. Chinese workers, who made up nearly half the world's factory workforce when the global decline began, became vastly more productive. Their wages rose. Their output soared. But the number of jobs fell.

In short, productivity ate the jobs. This diagnosis has profound implications for the policy prescription. Tariffs might change where some goods are made. But they won't change this underlying reality that the global economy now produces more manufactured goods with fewer factory workers.[37]

The problem isn't China stealing jobs. It's that factories just don't need as many workers as they used to. And that's not something a tariff can fix. To put it differently, US tariffs might succeed in reshoring some manufacturing work, but much of that will be done by industrial robots, not US workers.

The US experience: Jobs lost, blame misplaced

In the United States, the loss of manufacturing jobs has become political shorthand for decline, betrayal, and economic unfairness. Since the late 1970s, the US has shed nearly 7 million manufacturing jobs – falling from about 19 million in 1979 to just under 12 million today.[38] But here's the part rarely mentioned on the campaign trail: US manufacturing output didn't fall. It rose.

35 Baldwin, R. (2024, January 17). China is the world's sole manufacturing superpower: A line sketch of the rise. VoxEU (CEPR Policy Portal). https://cepr.org/voxeu/columns/china-worlds-sole-manufacturing-superpower-line-sketch-rise

36 Baldwin, R. (2024, January 17). China is the world's sole manufacturing superpower: A line sketch of the rise. VoxEU (CEPR Policy Portal). https://cepr.org/voxeu/columns/china-worlds-sole-manufacturing-superpower-line-sketch-rise

37 van Ark, B., & Monnikhof, E. (2000). Productivity and unit labour cost comparisons: A data base (Employment Paper 2000/5). International Labour Office. https://www.ilo.org/wcmsp5/groups/public/---ed_emp/documents/publication/wcms_142286.pdf

38 Harris, K. (2020, November). Forty years of falling manufacturing employment. Beyond the Numbers: Employment & Unemployment, 9(16). US Bureau of Labor Statistics. https://www.bls.gov/opub/btn/volume-9/forty-years-of-falling-manufacturing-employment.htm

What changed was productivity. American factories became more efficient. The remaining workers were producing more with less. This pattern mirrors the Agricultural Revolution that displaced millions of farm workers but didn't shrink the food supply. In fact, US manufacturing value added – how much factories contribute to GDP – hit record highs even as employment fell.

It wasn't trade that wiped out the factory floor. Studies, including those by the Congressional Budget Office and the Brookings Institution, estimate that trade with China (especially after its 2001 WTO entry) explains perhaps one-fifth to one-third of the job losses. The rest? Mostly machines and software – robots on the assembly line, computers in the back office. [39,40,41]

And let's be clear: these were not factory jobs in 1955. By the 2000s, many US manufacturing jobs were already under pressure – not from unfair foreign competition, but from American firms chasing productivity, scale, and shareholder value.

Yes, there were real losers. Communities hollowed out. Regional shocks were mishandled. But blaming it all on foreigners is not just inaccurate – it's misleading. The real story is one of structural transformation. The US moved from a factory economy to a service economy, just like every other advanced nation. That shift brought gains in wealth and efficiency but also left behind workers who had once expected manufacturing to provide stable, lifelong employment.

In short, Trump is right to care about manufacturing workers. But he's wrong to trust tariffs to do that.

Why Trump's tariffs won't reindustrialise America

Sometimes it seems like the Trump administration views tariffs as some sort of Marvel superpower for bringing manufacturing back home. And to be fair, tariffs can play a role in guiding industrial development in a country with a domestic market as large as that of the US. But let's be very clear about what they can't do: tariffs don't build.

Annex 1 illustrates this point by looking at two cases where tariff-led industrialisation did work in the old days, namely, the US in the 19th century and Korea in the 20th century. It also looks at how tariffs had almost nothing to do with the world's most spectacular industrialisation – that of China since 1995. Why was China different? Why has protectionism become destructionism when it comes to manufacturing?

39 Congressional Budget Office. (2024, December). Effects of illustrative policies that would increase tariffs (CBO Publication No. 61112). https://www.cbo.gov/system/files/2024-12/61112-Tariffs.pdf
40 Liu, J., & Woo, W. T. (2018, March 22). Understanding the US-China trade relationship. Brookings Institution. https://www.brookings.edu/articles/understanding-the-u-s-china-trade-relationship/
41 Scott, R. E., Mokhiber, Z., & Kimball, W. (2020, January 30). Growing China trade deficit cost 3.7 million American jobs between 2001 and 2018: Jobs lost in every US state and congressional district. Economic Policy Institute. https://www.epi.org/publication/growing-china-trade-deficits-costs-us-jobs/

The rise of global value chains (GVCs) fundamentally rewrote the playbook for industrialisation. In the past, tariffs were powerful tools for nurturing domestic industries – shielding them from foreign competition until they could achieve a critical mass. But GVCs shattered the old "infant industry protection" logic. With production now sliced across borders, tariffs no longer shield – they severe. They drive up costs, disrupt finely tuned supply chains, and scare off investment. That's why developing nations around the world rushed to unilaterally lower their tariffs in the 1990s. They had to if they wanted to attract factories offshored by G7 firms. In today's interconnected world, industrial success demands integration, not insulation. What once built factories now breaks them.

Tariffs protect, but they don't build

Tariffs don't coordinate investment across firms and sectors. They don't train workers. They don't bridge skill gaps or modernise vocational education. They don't fund infrastructure, improve logistics, or support research and development. They don't unlock capital, align upstream and downstream firms, or connect regions to supply chains. In short, tariffs can defend an industrial base, but they cannot create one.

Reindustrialisation requires more than tweaking relative prices. It needs a strategy. A real one. With planning, sequencing, and sustained commitment. It needs a trained workforce, one that matches the needs of 21st-century manufacturing.

And to get those workers, federal and local governments must partner with industry. Firms can't do it alone. No company will invest heavily in training workers if they're unsure those workers will stay once their skills are upgraded. That's why, in most countries, governments step in – funding training with tax dollars to solve the coordination problem. It's a public good with private benefits, and it only works when governments and employers pull in the same direction.

It also needs reliable infrastructure, stable regulation, and targeted investment incentives. It needs the trust of industrialists – not just that the cost of imported goods will be higher this year, but that America will be a profitable place to make things for decades to come.

And this is critical: building a modern manufacturing operation is a long-term proposition. From planning to permitting, from equipment procurement to workforce training, the timeline is measured in years, not months. For investors to commit, they need confidence that support policies – tariffs, subsidies, tax credits, training programmes – will remain in place long enough to generate a return. If the policy environment is unpredictable or politicised, those factories won't get built.

That's the real shortcoming of Trump's pray-and-spray, tariff-first and tariffs-only approach to reshoring manufacturing. There's no plan to use the breathing room tariffs might create. Without that plan, the most likely outcomes from the 2 April tariffs are higher prices, reduced manufacturing, riled allies, and retaliation against exports from industries where America is competitive today.

What might actually work

Tariffs can be a tool, but they are not a strategy. They are a slogan. If reindustrialisation is the goal, it requires investment, training, infrastructure, and coordination – not just import taxes.

The good news is that the US has begun rediscovering industrial policy. The CHIPS Act, the Inflation Reduction Act (IRA), and other Biden-era initiatives have laid out serious strategies to rebuild critical sectors – from semiconductors to green tech – using public–private coordination, targeted subsidies, and long-term planning.[42]

It is also good news that a key reality has been recognised (at least by the previous administration): America can't expand all manufacturing sectors at once. It needs to prioritise. And the goal shouldn't be to recreate the past, but to build future-facing industries that support both economic and national security.

In that effort, the US can learn from itself. Industrial policy works – when it's done right. Look at American agriculture – an area of globally competitive strength, built on a foundation of government-backed crop insurance, research support, infrastructure, and coordinated policy spanning decades.[43] Or take the defence sector, where government procurement, R&D funding, and planning created world-leading firms that wouldn't exist without the Pentagon's steady hand.[44]

In both cases, extensive and expensive public–private partnerships helped channel resources into sectors where the market alone wouldn't have delivered economic security, resilience, or military strength.

Reindustrialisation, if taken seriously, requires the same kind of sustained commitment. And it requires getting the details right – on workforce training, supply chain resilience, and targeted technological bets. If tariffs are the wall, then industrial policy must be the scaffolding that builds what's behind it. Without the latter, we're just leaning on slogans.

But the real question now is whether the Biden-era industrial policies – still in their early stages – will be allowed to mature, or whether the Trump administration will short-circuit them by downgrading investment, coordination, and training in favour of tariffs alone.

---

42 Hufbauer, G. C., Hogan, M., & Chen, M. (2025). Industrial policy through the CHIPS and Science Act: A preliminary report (PIIE Briefing 25-1). Peterson Institute for International Economics. https://www.piie.com/sites/default/files/2025-01/piieb25-1.pdf

43 Shields, D. A. (2015). Farm safety net programs: Background and issues (CRS Report No. R43758). Congressional Research Service. https://sgp.fas.org/crs/misc/R43758.pdf

44 Nicastro, L. A. (2024). The US defense industrial base: Background and issues for Congress (CRS Report No. R47751). Congressional Research Service. https://sgp.fas.org/crs/natsec/R47751.pdf

Summary and concluding remarks

President Trump is right about one big thing: America does need to reindustrialise. The loss of manufacturing capabilities – especially in strategically vital sectors – has left the nation economically exposed and, in some cases, militarily vulnerable. But while the diagnosis is broadly correct, the prescription is dangerously flawed.

Tariffs alone won't rebuild American industry. They don't train workers. They don't coordinate private investment. They don't create the infrastructure or innovation ecosystems that modern industry requires. At best, they protect; at worst, they backfire. As history has shown – repeatedly – import substitution without a serious industrial strategy often results in stagnation, not renewal.

What's changed now is that the "End of History dream" – the belief that open markets and global rules would guide all nations toward peaceful cooperation – has given way to a far more turbulent reality. Trade, investment, and supply chains are being weaponised. Tanks are crossing borders to redraw maps, as if it were 1938. And even beyond man-made geopolitical risks, the world faces systemic shocks – pandemics, climate change, cyberattacks – that remind us how fragile global interdependence can be.

In this world, it no longer seems wise – or safe – to entrust manufacturing entirely to the invisible hand of global markets. Leaders across the world are rethinking industrial strategy. Reshoring, near-shoring, and friend-shoring have become the new pillars of economic resilience. From Brussels to Tokyo to Washington, the conversation has shifted. It's not just about efficiency anymore. It's about security, stability, and sovereignty.

The most important flaw in the Trump administration's thinking about these issues is their lack of patience, and go-it-alone, top-down approach.

Reindustrialisation is not a bumper-sticker issue. It's a generational project that requires planning, public–private coordination, and long-term investment. The United States has done it before – in sectors like agriculture and defence – where sustained government support helped forge globally competitive industries. It can be done again. But it won't be done with tariffs alone, and it won't be done quickly. A stable, bipartisan coalition is needed to underpin the decades-long plans that private firms will have to make to accomplish the mission.

America's industrial future won't be made with walls and slogans. It will be made with patient policy, strategic investment, and the hard, unglamorous work of rebuilding capabilities that were lost through decades of neglect and drift.

In short: the goal is right. But to reach it, the US needs real tools, not just real anger.

6   Tariffs can't fix trade deficits

The myth at the heart of Trump's trade policy

Donald Trump's return to the tariff pulpit in 2025 has revived one of the most persistent economic myths of our time: that tariffs can fix America's trade deficit. On the campaign trail he repeatedly promised to enact a 10% tariff on all trade partners and all products, and a higher rate of 60% on Chinese imports.

But here's the truth. Tariffs cannot and will not fix the US trade deficit. They never have. And they never will because trade balances are not about trade policy, they are about economy-wide imbalances.

The reason America is buying more from foreigners than foreigners are buying from America is because America is spending more than America produces. So, how do you think America satisfies the excess demand? It does so by importing more than it exports. In short, a trade deficit is the mirror image of a macroeconomic imbalance. Since tariffs cannot fix the macroeconomic imbalance, tariffs cannot fix the deficit.

Admittedly that assertion may not strike all readers as self-evident. That's why this chapter unpacks that idea. We'll walk through the basic logic. We'll illustrate it with what I like to call the "secret formula" of trade balances. We'll explain how Trump's tariffs can affect who the US runs a deficit with, but not whether it runs one at all. And we'll end with a grim prediction: if Trump proceeds as planned, the US trade deficit will likely get worse, not better. And this leads to the disturbing thought that he might try something even more radical to rebalance trade.

Why it seems like tariffs should work

President Trump has long believed that tariffs can rebalance the US trade deficit. On the surface, this sounds perfectly reasonable. After all, if America is buying more from abroad than it sells, why not just tax the imports and shrink the gap? It's a compelling idea.

It taps into a deep economic instinct: if you don't like your balance, tax what you're buying. It's also entirely wrong, but let's first discuss why it seems so right.

Everyone knows about how taxes can change what you buy. People see it in their everyday shopping. When, the governments put up "sin taxes" on things like cigarettes and alcohol, people tend to buy less of them. When the price of gasoline goes up, people tend to buy less and drive less (to the extent that's possible).

How can this economic logic seem so reasonable and be so wrong? The source of the misthinking is all down to thinking about only one side of the story. The trade deficit depends on two things, not just one. Tariffs can only help with one of those, but – as it turns out – it is the other one that is determinant.

The two-handed truth in theory and fables

The trade balance is moved by two levers: one is an economy-wide imbalance, and the other is the price difference between domestic and foreign goods. Let's take a closer look at each.

One lever – let's call it the "right-hand lever" – is the one everyone's familiar with. It's the obvious driver of trade. People encounter it all the time at the store, comparing the price tags on local products versus imports. This lever works at the level of individual products, like shoes, beer, and vegetables. You put a tariff on foreign goods, their prices go up, people buy fewer imports and switch to domestic stuff.

But there's a second lever controlling the trade deficit – the one that is almost always overlooked, including by President Trump and his advisors.

Let's call this second one the "left-hand lever". The left-hand lever operates at the economy-wide level, not at the level of shoes, beer, and vegetables like the right-hand lever. The left-hand lever is the imbalance between US spending and US production. It is simple, and obvious really, once you shift your focus from shoes, beer, and vegetables to what's going on at the level of the whole economy.

If US residents and companies spend more than is produced inside the borders of America, there will not be enough American-made stuff to fulfil the demand. Where do you think US residents and companies will get the stuff to cover their excess spending? The answer is obvious and inevitable. They get it by importing more than they export.

To reframe this in terms of imbalance, the spending–production gap is an economy-wide imbalance between spending and production, which has to be made up by imported foreign things. Note that for the economy as a whole, the value of America's total domestic production exactly equals its total domestically produced income. The technical name for this income/production is gross domestic product (GDP).

Now, to take the left-hand lever for a road test, to get you familiar with it, try to imagine how the spending–income gap could exist without being matched by the trade gap. Can you find another way to fill that gap that doesn't involve foreign goods and services? You can't.

An economy-wide spending-versus-production imbalance must be matched – always, everywhere, and perfectly – by the net purchase of foreign goods, that is to say, by the trade deficit.

In a nutshell, and to repeat myself since repetition is what professors do for a living, the left-hand lever is the equality between the spending–income gap and the import–export gap.

This isn't theory. It isn't some globalist talking point. It's accounting. It's arithmetic. Every dollar the US spends beyond its GDP (in other words, beyond what it produces domestically) gets matched – perfectly and automatically – by a dollar of US trade deficit. Always and everywhere.

The reason the left-hand lever is not widely understood is not due to its complexity, it is due to its visibility. Because it operates at the economy-wide level, it is harder to spot. After all, people don't walk around thinking about GDP or what all Americans are spending versus what they are earning. People have better things to do. They have enough problems dealing with their own slice of the economy.

But once you've been alerted to the left-hand, economy-wide lever, the logic is just as clear as the right-hand lever. To repeat: if Americans – households, firms, and the government – spend more than the country produces, that gap has to be filled somehow. And the only way to fill it is by importing goods, on net, from foreigners.

To fix the deficit the US must pull both levers; tariffs alone won't work

So, if America wants to fix its trade deficit, it must pull both levers. It has to shift the relative price of foreign and domestic goods (that's the right-hand lever), and here tariffs can help. But it must also address the economy-wide imbalance between spending and production (the left-hand lever). Or to rephrase it, America must fix its economy-wide spending–income imbalance and make domestic goods more attractive if it wants to fix its deficit.

That brings us to the crux of the matter. The point that President Trump misses. Tariffs can pull the right-hand lever – they can nudge prices. But tariffs can't touch the left-hand lever. They can't fix an economy-wide overspending problem. And unless both levers move, the trade deficit won't budge.

The two-handed truth in fables

Don't worry if all this sounds like the sort of reasoning that gives economists a bad name. If that's how you feel, you are in good company. To get past this, let me try a different tack. I'll use stories. There is nothing juvenile about teaching complex lessons with stories. The most influential books in the world, holy books, are a list of stories.

Story No.1: Teenagers with credit cards

Picture this: teenagers with credit cards, small incomes, and zero budgeting skills. Every month, they spend more than they earn – new shoes, takeout dinners, streaming subscriptions, you name it. The result? Their credit card balance keeps rising. That's their version of a trade deficit.

In economic terms, the teens have a spending–income imbalance. And just like with the US trade balance, that gap has to be filled somehow. For the teens, it's filled by borrowing more or leaning on the bank of mum and dad. For the US, it's filled by importing more than the US exports. Either way, the logic is ironclad: a gap between what you spend and what you make always leads to a growing deficit – on the card, or on the trade ledger.

So how do you fix it? Well, there are really only two levers: spend less, or earn more.

But that is not what's happening when tariffs are used to fix the trade deficit. Here's the analogy with the spendthrift teenagers.

Imagine their parents told them to only shop at fancy, high-priced stores, and only buy takeout from the most expensive restaurants. This will shift the relative price between spending and not spending. And sure, that might slow them down a little. But here's the real problem. This doesn't actually fix the core problem that they're still spending more than they make.

Recommending more expensive stores is like using tariffs to solve America's trade deficit. Yes, behaviour might shift slightly. But the root problem – the mismatch between income and spending – is untouched. And unless you pull both levers, nothing really changes.

Here is another fable that makes the right-hand and left-hand point.

Story No. 2: The village that knew the secret trade balance formula

Once upon a time, in the Kingdom of Econia, there were two villages called Balanceburg and Tariff Town. These villages traded with one another and with other villages, swapping sugar for shoes and copper for cloth. The Elders in each village were absolutely sure that they understood the forces that governed trade deficits.

In Tariff Town, the Elders believed in a simple and powerful idea: "The trade balance is just exports minus imports. So, if there's a deficit, imports must be the problem." To them, the solution to a trade deficit was obvious. "If we're importing too much, we'll just make imports more expensive!"

So they raised tariffs – first on sugar, then on cloth, then on everything they could think of. But no matter how high the tariffs climbed, the trade deficit refused to disappear. It was as if something else – something unseen – was at play.

Meanwhile, over in Balanceburg, the Elders had a broader view of what drives the trade deficit. Their ancestors, you see, had long ago discovered the "secret formula" for the trade balance. Of course, they knew the public formula that was used in Tariff Town, but they also had the secret formula, which said that the trade balance equalled – always, everywhere, and perfectly – the difference between the village's spending and the village's income.

When Balanceburg's trade account dipped into the red, they did not impose taxes on foreign goods. They just spent less. And when their trade swung too far into surplus, they spent a bit more. Their trade balance stayed remarkably steady – not because they taxed their way to balance, but because they understood which levers they needed to pull.

The strangest thing is that Balanceburg did nothing to keep the formula secret. It was carved into stone in the town square and printed on the village flag: "Trade balance equals spending minus income." But the formula stayed secret because no one else believed it was true. They couldn't understand what spending and income could possibly have to do with a trade balance.

The Tariff Town Elders, meanwhile, kept yanking on the same lever – prices of imports – expecting everything else to fall in line. But it never did. The truth was simple: tariffs could tug the right-hand lever – relative prices – but they couldn't move the left-hand lever – the gap between what the village spent and what it earned. And until both levers were understood and used together, Tariff Town's deficits were never going to disappear.

The secret formula is fine in theory, but does it work in practice?

Having heard the fairy tales and read the theory, you will be wondering whether all this holds in reality. Is it true that the trade deficit exactly, always, and perfectly matches the spending–income gap?

The chart below shows the secret formula for the United States for all the quarters from 2022 to 2024. The left bars show America's net imports in billions of dollars. The right bars show the imbalance between American spending and production in billions of dollars.

Did you notice the two gaps – the spending–income gap and the import–export gap – are *exactly* the same? They are identical. Not just correlated. Not just about the same. They are the same number down to the last decimal point. That's the secret formula in action.

THE SECRET FORMULA FOR THE US BALANCE OF TRADE (US$ BILLIONS)

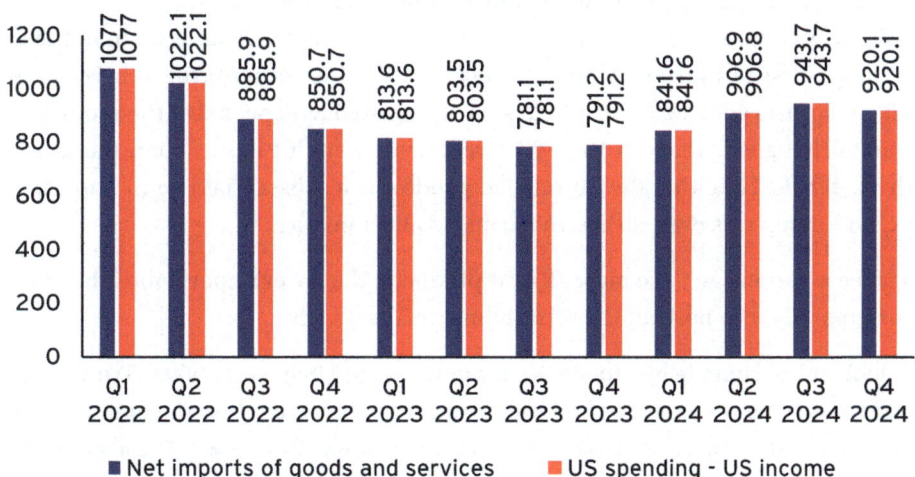

Source: US Bureau of Economic Analysis[1]

Note: "US spending - US income" is the difference between sum of Personal consumption expenditure + Gross private domestic investments + Government consumption expenditure and gross investments and GDP

1   US Bureau of Economic Analysis. (2025). National Data: GDP & Personal Income [Data set] (Table 1.1.5). US Department of Commerce. Retrieved April 30, 2025

If you skipped the story of the teenagers and the story of Tariff Town and Balanceburg, you may find it weird that the two imbalances are identical. How could that be? Is it a coincidence?

There is no mystery. Just reality. If America spends more than it produces, the spending–production gap has to be filled by the net import of foreign goods.

Now you know the secret formula. But little good it'll do you. Having tried to teach this point for almost 40 years, and having watched my fellow, more competent colleagues do the same, I've found that the secret formula remains secret because the secret keeps itself.

Go ahead. Try to explain it to your pub pals that the trade deficit equals the imbalance between America's spending and its income. My guess is that they won't believe you, and you'll see why it has remained a secret for so long from people as worldly as the President of the United States of America.

The stories above are about how the two gaps match, so both levers must be pulled. But what is the economic mechanism linking the two gaps – the two levers, so to speak. The next story provides the answer.

Exchange rates offset trade policy

This section turns to three real world examples where movements in the value of the currency offset the impact of trade policy changes. The first is the most relevant, so be sure you don't skip it.

What did tariffs do to the deficit in Trump's first term?

Tariffs reduce imports. Tariffs are, after all, a tax on imports. That is plain in the data. In Trump's first term, some Chinese exports to the US got no tariff, others got a 7% tariff, and others got a 25% tariff.[2,3] The tariffs worked as expected at the product level. The imported goods that got the 25% "treatment" were hit harder than those treated with 7% tariffs. Note that the un-tariffed goods saw a substantial rise in imports once the Covid slump was over. So clearly tariffs do affect imports.

But since a nation can't use more than it produces, the lower imports must be offset by lower exports. Or to pull out the refrain: macro always wins.

Just look at the chart below to see what happened to US exports when Trump started his trade war in 2018. Covid-19 and the resulting recession confuse the data from 2020, but in 2018 and 2019, we see that first US imports slows, and US exports also slowed.

2   Bown, C. P. (2025, April 12). US-China trade war tariffs: An up-to-date chart. Peterson Institute for International Economics. https://www.piie.com/research/piie-charts/2019/us-china-trade-war-tariffs-date-chart

3   Bekkers, E., & Schroeter, S. (2020, March 19). An economic analysis of the US-China trade conflict (WTO Staff Working Paper ERSD-2020-04). World Trade Organization. https://www.wto.org/english/res_e/reser_e/ersd202004_e.pdf

While tariffs can affect only the relative-price determinant of trade deficit – which is to say, macro always wins – bilateral tariffs can affect bilateral trade balances. Bilateral tariffs can shift the imbalance from one trade partner to another.

US EXPORTS AND IMPORTS OF GOODS AND SERVICES, BALANCE OF PAYMENTS BASIS (CURRENT US$ BILLIONS)

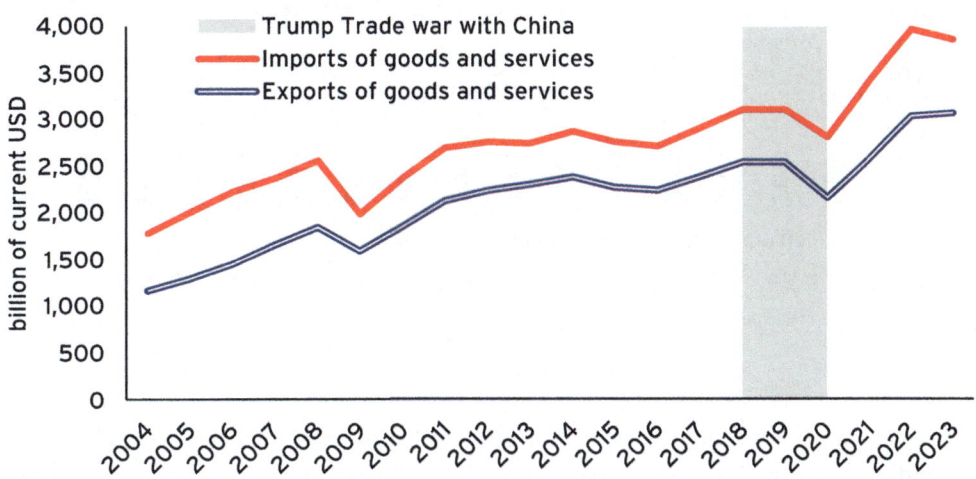

Source: World Bank's WDI database[4]

Note: Exports and imports of goods and services are in current USD prices (series BM.GSR.GNFS.CD, BX.GSR.GNFS.CD)

The next chart shows that the first Trump administration's tariffs did affect the US–China bilateral deficit, but not the overall trade balance. Recall that China retaliated so US exports to China were hit, and Chinese exports to the US were hit. The diamond-marker line shows that the bilateral deficit with China was growing up till Trump started the trade war in March 2018, and then it became less negative.

You can also see that the deficit with everyone else got worse, more or less one for one, during the trade war. The overall US trade deficit was heading south for macroeconomic reasons. Macro, in short, won the day.

4   World Bank. (2024). World Development Indicators. https://databank.worldbank.org/source/world-development-indicators

US TRADE BALANCE, TOTAL AND BILATERAL WITH CHINA

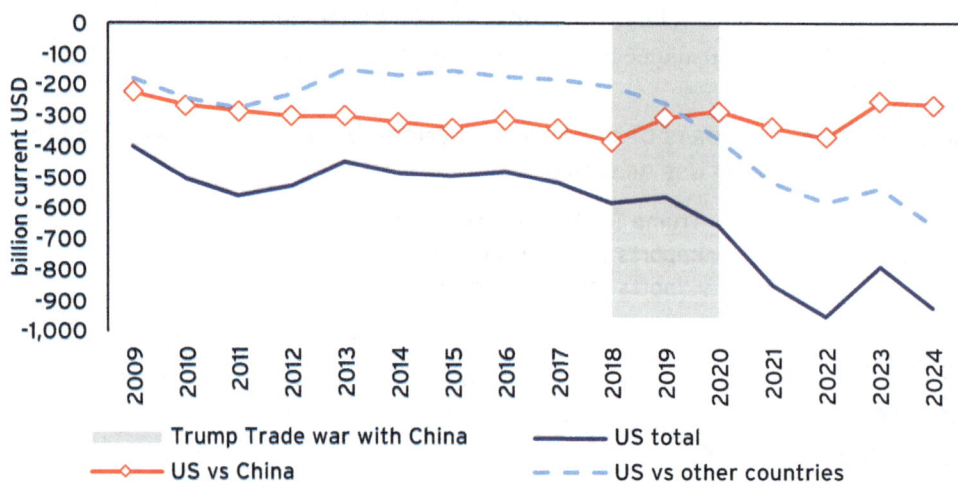

Source: US Bureau of Economic Analysis.[5]

Note: trade balance is net balance on goods and services.

There are other revealing cases where tariffs failed to reduce trade deficits, but since they disrupt the logical flow of the chapter, I've gathered them in Annex 2 for readers interested in exploring them further.

Why is the dollar going up and down?

This chapter has been explaining how a broad-based tariff should strengthen the dollar in a way that lowers exports to match the lower imports. It does this since the dollar movement is necessary to ensure the spending–income gap continues to match the export–import gap.

But by the third week of April 2025, the headlines were saying the opposite: the dollar was falling in a way that seemed to contradict the prediction that a stronger dollar would offset the tariffs' impact on the trade deficit.[6,7] So, what happened?

In late 2024 and early 2025, the dollar did, as expected, gain value when Trump's election was announced. At this moment, the market narrative was clear: tariffs would raise prices and tax cuts would raise US demand. The Fed would raise interest rates to tame inflation and avoid overheating. Higher-than-expected interest rates would make dollar-denominated assets more attractive. More demand for dollars means a stronger

5   US Bureau of Economic Analysis. (2025). Table 1.5. US International Trade in Goods and Services by Area and Country [Data set]. US Department of Commerce. https://apps.bea.gov/international/bp_web/tb_download_type_modern.cfm?list=1&RowID=30164

6   CNBC. (2025, April 21). US dollar falls to three-year low as Trump's Powell threats further dent investor confidence. Retrieved from https://www.cnbc.com/2025/04/21/us-dollar-falls-to-three-year-low-as-trumps-powell-threats-further-dent-investor-confidence.html.

7   Reuters. (2025, April 24). Dollar has further to fall, says Goldman Sachs chief economist. Retrieved from https://www.reuters.com/business/finance/dollar-has-further-fall-says-goldman-sachs-chief-economist-2025-04-24/

dollar. And that's what we saw: from October to February, the dollar appreciated steadily.

But by March, the narrative flipped. Trump's trade policy turned erratic, as the previous chapter pointed out. The president ripped up all of America's trade agreements and the promises it made at the WTO. Exemptions were granted, then revoked. Allies were hit with, or threatened with, unexpectedly high tariffs. The US and China jumped into a spiral of retaliation that drove bilateral tariffs up to business-destroying level. As pointed out in the last chapter, the world had never seen trade policy that was this erratic.[8] It was scary to watch. And the foreign exchange market does not like scary.

Moreover, while the inflationary aspects of the tariffs were clear, the uncertainty was leading people to hesitate on buying durable goods like cars and household appliances.[9] And it led companies to postpone investments. The combination reduced aggregate demand, and this lowered growth projections.

When the markets soured on US growth prospects, they started to think about stagflation and instability. Instead of the Fed hiking rates, they began to expect the Fed to cut them.[10] And that changed everything.

When markets expect US interest rates to fall, dollar assets become less attractive. Capital flows reverse. The dollar weakens. This wasn't a minor adjustment. It was a full narrative pivot – from boom to bust. And the dollar fell accordingly.

All these rapid-fire changes in expectations did not, indeed could not, change the necessity of the trade balance offsetting the spending–income imbalance. But now the exchange rate didn't have to rise to neutralise the impact of the tariffs. The US slowdown was expected to do that. A recession, after all, would reduce US spending more than income, as it usually does. This would lower the gap that the trade deficit needed to match, so tariffs wouldn't need to be offset. The secret formula for the trade balance, as I called it, was expected to hold and reduced demand would do the work. In short, the method of adjustment changed. The pending slowdown did the matching that a stronger dollar would have had to do without the contractionary tendency.

Once the recession passes, as it surely will, the US will be back to the standard logic and the dollar will have to appreciate.

To sum up, markets bought the "growth and inflation" story in January. They bought dollars. But by April, they had switched to the "chaos and recession" story. They sold dollars – and bought safety.

---

8   Davis, S. J. (2025, April 23). *Destructive trade policy* [Panel discussion paper]. Hoover Institution Economic Policy Working Group. https://stevenjdavis.com/s/Destructive-Trade-Policy-23-April-2025.pdf

9   Oxford Analytica. (2025, April 29). Tariff uncertainty will damage the US retail sector. Retrieved May 1, 2025, from https://www.oxan.com/insights/tariff-uncertainty-will-damage-the-us-retail-sector/

10 Saphir, A. (2025, April 30). Fed signals rates will remain unchanged despite market bets on looming cuts. Reuters. Retrieved May 1, 2025, from https://www.reuters.com/business/traders-pare-bets-fed-rate-cuts-2025-still-see-june-start-2025-04-30/

The result? The US trade deficit will shrink, but not because of the tariffs directly. It will shrink because the tariff chaos is likely to induce a recession that will reduce the deficit.

Summary and concluding remarks

The US president is promising to fix the trade deficit with tariffs. This won't work. The idea that tariffs can cure a trade deficit has enduring political appeal. It feels intuitive. It looks decisive. It gives the appearance of action. But as we've seen – through logic, data, historical analogies, and a couple of fables – this belief is mistaken. Worse, it's dangerously misleading.

Trade deficits are not primarily the result of unfair foreign competition. They are the mirror image of domestic choices. They arise when a nation consumes and invests more than it produces – when it spends more than it earns. That gap must be financed somehow. And in an open economy, that "somehow" is the trade deficit.

To be clear, this means that the trade balance is not determined by trade policy. It is determined by the macroeconomics. Until the macroeconomic imbalance shifts, the overall trade deficit will not budge. As we saw in Trump's first term, tariffs can influence who the US runs a deficit with, but not whether it runs one at all.

In this chapter, we've walked through the arithmetic of adjustment, illustrated the logic through metaphors, and shown how the exchange rate acts as an automatic stabiliser. We saw this in the first Trump tariff war, in the Dutch Disease aftermath of America's fracking boom, and in the Brexit example (see the Annex). Time and again, the lesson repeats: macro always wins.

To be clear, tariffs can and do change trade flows. They create sectoral winners and losers. They may even be justified in narrow strategic contexts. But they do not change the overall trade balance unless they also change the nation's savings and investment patterns. Tariffs lower both imports and exports.

Closing remarks: What happens when tariffs don't fix the deficit?
Recessions are one of the most reliable ways of fixing a trade deficit – in the US and elsewhere. US growth is slowing, and the country might slip into a recession, but that won't last forever. This raises a disturbing possibility.

Once the "Trump-cession" passes, the trade deficit will return. Indeed, since the administration's policies promise to cut taxes more than government spending, the imbalance between what the US spends and what it earns is likely to grow. The growth in the spending–income gap will, as we saw in many ways, have to be matched with a larger trade deficit.

Here are two disturbing thoughts. First, what if the Trump administration continues to believe that tariffs will fix the deficit and concludes that what is needed is even higher tariffs? Another disturbing thought is that if tariffs don't improve the trade deficit,

Trump may seek other solutions. One possibility is the Miran memo – sometimes dubbed the "Mar-a-Lago Accord". This controversial memo by Stephan Miran,[11] who is now the Chairman of President Trump's Council of Economic Advisors, seeks ways to engineer a dollar depreciation, like the 1985 Plaza Accord. It is quite crazy, as many economists have pointed out.[12]

The memo outlines a scheme for reducing the American deficit by making the dollar so unattractive that it plummets. The plan envisions this dollar fall as being severe enough to reduce the US spending–income gap and the export–import gap along with it. Such measures could severely destabilise the global economy.

The severity of the dollar and bond sell-off following the 2 April tariffs provides some hope that the Miran memo policy will not be tried. The president, after all, backed down on 9 April to end the turmoil that had started to spin out of control in the US Treasury market. This suggested that the White House now recognises the potential for economic disaster if the creditworthiness of the dollar is jeopardised. This episode reduces the likelihood of Miran's Mar-a-Lago Accord being implemented. However, Trump's unpredictability means no option can be entirely ruled out.

In any case, countries should start thinking ahead on the possibility that the Miran memo policies will be tried in an attempt to correct the persistent US trade deficit. The disruption could happen at the speed of the Global Financial Crisis of 2008-09. Plans should be made in advance to respond swiftly and decisively to extreme disruptions that could ripple across global financial markets. Strategic clarity today could help prevent economic chaos tomorrow.

11 Miran, S. (2024, November). A user's guide to restructuring the global trading system [PDF]. Hudson Bay Capital Management LP. https://www.hudsonbaycapital.com/documents/FG/hudsonbay/research/638199_A_Users_Guide_to_Restructuring_the_Global_Trading_System.pdf
12 Chinn, M. (2025, January 6). Miran's manifesto. Econbrowser. Retrieved May 1, 2025, from https://econbrowser.com/archives/2025/01/mirans-manifesto

7 The US–China conflict is not a trade war
The dangerous illusion that a systems clash can be won

The Trump administration characterises the US–China conflict as a trade war that can be fought with the tools the president's Great Trade Hack is using (tariffs). But this is a fundamental misunderstanding of the nature of the conflict.

Focusing on imports, exports, and supply chains obscures the fact that this is not a traditional trade war – it is a systems clash. The underlying struggle is not about trade flows, but about a clash between two very different forms of capitalism: America's market-led capitalism and China's state-led capitalism.

This means the conflict is not really about the levels of tariffs, subsidies, or government procurement. It is rooted in much deeper differences between the governments' economic objectives, the tools they use to pursue them, their visions of what a prosperous society looks like, and their broader worldviews.

These systemic differences have existed for decades, but the conflict has become top-of-mind in Washington because China's model has proven particularly successful – culminating in its rise as the world's sole manufacturing superpower.[1] This is why many in America are now viewing Beijing's model as a threat.

The danger lies in how this threat is being misdiagnosed as a conventional trade war by the Trump administration. This mischaracterisation creates the illusion that the conflict can be "won".

This is a dangerous illusion.

A systems clash is not a zero-sum contest with a final score. It is a long-term rivalry over values, institutions, and economic direction. The goal cannot be victory – it must be strategic coexistence.

This chapter first explains why the US–China conflict is a systems clash that neither side can win, then turns to historical lessons from America's last systems clash – with Japan in the 1980s. It concludes by applying those lessons to how the current US–China confrontation might be managed.

Why the US–China conflict is a systems clash

The US–China rivalry stems from two fundamentally different models of capitalism. The American system is rooted in decentralised decision-making, lightly regulated

---

1   Baldwin, R. (2024, January 17). China is the world's sole manufacturing superpower: A line sketch of the rise. VoxEU (CEPR Policy Portal). https://cepr.org/voxeu/columns/china-worlds-sole-manufacturing-superpower-line-sketch-rise

markets, and private-sector leadership. In contrast, China operates a state-led model where the government guides industrial priorities, allocates capital strategically, and integrates economic policy with political authority. These models are not technical variations; they are deeply embedded, coherent systems designed to produce national prosperity in very different ways.

In practical terms, these systems deploy distinct tools. The US relies on market incentives, open competition, and flexible labour and capital markets. China, meanwhile, uses subsidies, state-owned enterprises, directed credit, and industrial plans like "Made in China 2025" to advance strategic sectors. The friction between the two arises not just from economic outcomes, but from incompatible views of what legitimate economic policy looks like. Each side sees the other's approach as violating the rules or spirit of global economic order.

This divergence becomes most evident in areas like semiconductors, artificial intelligence, electric vehicles, and 5G. These are not just sectors; they are the commanding heights of 21st-century economic power. The US views China's gains in these areas as not just commercial advances but strategic threats. China, for its part, views US export controls and investment restrictions as attempts to suppress its development. The result is not a dispute over trade balances, but a strategic rivalry for technological leadership.

To be sure, these systemic differences have existed for decades. But they have become harder to ignore as China's model has grown more successful – and more assertive. Its rise as the world's leading manufacturing power has changed the global economic map and challenged assumptions built into US policy. This transformation explains why the US no longer sees China as just a trade partner or economic rival, but as a systemic challenger to its economic worldview.

Why neither side can win this systems clash

Neither side in this systems clash can expect the other to capitulate or convert. Winning is an illusion. Indeed, as of early May 2025, it looked like Trump's trade Hack was seriously backfiring – causing unsustainable harm to the US economy but sustainable harm to the Chinese economy.

China will not dismantle its state-led model, which is deeply entwined with national identity, political control, and economic strategy. For the Chinese Communist Party, abandoning this model would be tantamount to surrendering legitimacy. Likewise, the United States will not shift toward state-led capitalism or relinquish its commitment to open markets and democratic pluralism. Each system is too deeply rooted in its own ideological, institutional, and historical foundations to be dislodged by pressure from abroad.

Even if one side sought confrontation, economic interdependence creates enormous incentives for escalation. The two economies are tightly interwoven through supply chains, investment, and trade in intermediate goods. China is a critical supplier of components across US industries, while American firms are embedded in Chinese markets. Attempting a full decoupling would be slow, costly, and highly disruptive. The complexity of modern economic linkages – what some call the "omelette" problem – makes it extremely difficult, indeed impossible, to unscramble the omlette back into the separate eggs.

Although the US and China are interdependent, the balance of leverage is shifting. China is now less reliant on Western markets than it once was, and in many advanced manufacturing sectors the US is more dependent on Chinese inputs than vice versa. This asymmetry undermines the assumption that the US can use economic coercion to bend China to its will. Instead, attempts at pressure often backfire, exposing vulnerabilities in the US economy and encouraging Beijing to accelerate its drive for self-sufficiency.

The political immovable objects

Political reasons are piled on top of the economic reasons that tell us neither side can win or be seen as winning. Both Beijing and Washington are locked into domestic narratives that make reforming their systems unthinkable.

The problems in Washington are not as complicated as those in Beijing. Understanding the Chinese view requires as glance back to the time, a century ago, when trade war was settled with real war. In China, memories of Western imperialism and the "Century of Humiliation" foster a powerful aversion to external pressure and perceived subjugation. National pride makes capitulation politically impossible.

For Chinese policymakers, foreign "bullying" is not some vague threat – it is a searing national memory. The Opium Wars of the 19th century saw British gunboats on the Pearl River and troops marching through Chinese cities. Chinese ports were seized, and the British withdrew only when China signed the so-called "unequal treaties" that sapped its sovereignty and pride. This marked the beginning of what Chinese schoolchildren learn to call the "Century of Humiliation".

The trigger for British aggression has an eerie resonance with Donald Trump's obsession over bilateral trade deficits. In the early 19th century, Britain developed an enormous appetite for Chinese tea, silk, and porcelain, but China, adhering to mercantilist principles, insisted on payment in silver. To stem the outflow of silver, the British East India Company began smuggling opium from India into China, selling it for silver, and using that silver to purchase Chinese goods. The resulting addiction crisis led the Qing Dynasty to ban opium imports more strictly. When Chinese officials destroyed opium stocks in Canton, Britain launched a military response, compelling China to accept opium as payment through force.

To grasp the moral absurdity of this episode, imagine China today using military force to compel the US to accept fentanyl as payment for Boeing jets. This legacy of humiliation is not abstract; it informs China's response to US pressure today. Beijing sees tariffs, export bans, and investment restrictions not as isolated policy tools, but as echoes of past coercion. In this context, yielding to American demands would not only be seen as economically costly – it would be a surrender of dignity.

The US is caught in a political trap of its own. With its bipartisan consensus that blames China for the middle-class woes, America has painted itself into a corner.

Over the last two decades, blaming China for America's middle-class economic malaise has become a bipartisan sport. From Donald Trump's raucous 2016 rallies to Joe Biden's "Buy American" initiatives, scepticism of China now unites Democrats and Republicans alike.

Given this political landscape, no US president can easily afford to de-escalate the conflict without being accused of weakness. Any perceived "capitulation" would trigger fierce backlash – from Congress, from voters, and from influential industry lobbies. Washington's domestic political machinery has shifted from viewing China as a partner to viewing it as a threat. That shift is sticky, and it sharply narrows the room for pragmatic diplomacy.

This political deadlock means that the economic logic of mutual gain – so powerful in theory – often is getting buried under nationalist narratives, historical grievances, and electoral incentives. In a systems clash like this, where the stakes are as much about pride and identity as about money, allowing the other side to be seen as "winning" becomes politically impossible. Even a face-saving compromise would be a hard sell on both sides.

No US president can easily de-escalate the conflict without being accused of weakness. Any perceived "capitulation" would provoke backlash – from Congress, voters, and industry lobbies. Washington's political machinery has shifted from viewing China as a strategic partner to viewing it as a threat. That shift is deeply entrenched, narrowing the scope for pragmatic diplomacy.

This political deadlock on both sides means that the economic logic of mutual gain – so powerful in theory – is often buried beneath nationalist narratives, historical grievances, and electoral incentives. In a clash where pride and identity loom as large as policy and profit, even face-saving compromises become politically toxic. This is why neither side can win – and why managing the rivalry, rather than resolving it, is the only realistic path forward.

What can we learn from the last systems clash (the US-Japan conflict)

In the 1980s, Washington was gripped by a familiar fear: that a fast-rising industrial rival was overtaking key sectors – autos, semiconductors, and steel – while running a massive trade surplus with the United States. The rival wasn't China, but Japan.

I had the privilege of witnessing firsthand the final stages of this struggle from within the walls of the White House, under the Bush Senior administration in 1990-91. There are several useful lessons to take from the US–Japan systems clash for the US–China systems clash, but one important difference. In the 1980s and early 1990s, no one was talking about winning. Japan was a key military ally and an important pillar in America's East Asian security infrastructure. The goal was, if you allow the analogy, to remove the irritant, not cut out the eye.

Japan's rise was driven by a state-influenced, export-oriented model that delivered high-quality manufactured goods at competitive prices. American anxieties over declining industrial competitiveness soon morphed into political pressure. Japan was accused of unfair trade practices – ranging from a deliberately undervalued yen to opaque regulatory barriers.

The conflict was cast not just in commercial terms, but also as a systems clash. Japanese capitalism organised around corporate groupings known as keiretsu and close state–business ties, clashed with America's more market-driven ethos. US officials viewed these structures as distorting competition and undermining free trade.

The Reagan administration's response was a blend of hard and soft tactics. Voluntary export restraints capped Japanese car exports. Bilateral deals pried open Japanese markets for American goods. Aggressive trade laws like Super 301 threatened penalties for unfair trade in semiconductors and telecoms.

Perhaps the most consequential intervention came through monetary diplomacy. The 1985 Plaza Accord – signed by the US, Japan, and other major economies – engineered a sharp appreciation of the yen. This made Japanese exports more expensive and reduced the US trade deficit.

Japan, crucially, was a US ally. It responded with cooperation: accepting currency revaluation, expanding imports, and voluntarily limiting some exports. These gestures eased tensions. Yet accommodation alone did not resolve the rivalry.

Japan's internal vulnerabilities also played a decisive role. In the early 1990s, its asset bubble burst, plunging the country into decades of economic stagnation. As Japan slowed, the US shifted its attention to a new rising power – China. The creation of the WTO in 1995 further institutionalised global trade rules, helping to manage frictions.

The US–Japan conflict did not end with a clear winner. It faded through a mix of structural change, political alignment, and multilateral integration. The systems clash was never truly resolved, but the two countries found a way to coexist.

Key takeaways and lessons for today's clash

Several lessons stand out. Managed trade tools helped contain tensions, but monetary realignment and domestic economic shifts played a greater role. Japan's alliance with the US also smoothed the path to compromise – a condition which is not present in the US–China case.

The comparison with China highlights key differences. Japan exported finished goods and was only modestly embedded in US supply chains. China, by contrast, supplies intermediate goods across a broad spectrum of industries, making decoupling more costly and complex.

China is also a strategic competitor, not a compliant ally. Its response to US pressure has not been to accommodate but to harden, promoting self-sufficiency, diversifying export markets, and accelerating indigenous innovation. Policies like "dual circulation" signal China's resolve to reduce external dependence.

The lesson is not that Japan's case offers a blueprint, but that it offers useful cautions. Pragmatism, realism, and institutional guardrails helped prevent escalation in the 1980s. The same mindset is needed now.

If the US–China clash is to end as well as the clash with Japan, dreams of decisive victory must give way to the sober work of coexistence. America's success will depend not on weakening China's system, but on strengthening its own – and building stable, rules-based mechanisms to manage systemic competition over the long haul.

How could the US-China systems clash be managed?

If victory is off the table, what is left is the harder, less dramatic work of managing the US–China systems clash. That means shifting from a mindset of triumph to one of strategic endurance. Instead of seeking submission or systemic change, Washington must pursue a path of structured coexistence. The conflict can't be ended – but it can be stabilised.

- Set realistic objectives.

The US must abandon the fantasy that it can coerce China into abandoning its model of state-led capitalism. Rather than demanding sweeping systemic reforms, Washington should target specific, achievable outcomes: protecting critical technologies, improving transparency in subsidies, securing access to key markets, and ensuring reciprocal investment protections. Fixating on shrinking the bilateral trade deficit or blocking China's technological progress creates moving goalposts that only raise tensions.

- Accept systemic difference.

Like the US–Japan clash of the 1980s, the US–China rivalry involves two different economic logics. But unlike Japan, China will not be pressured into alignment with US preferences. Its model is strategic, nationalistic, and permanent. The US must stop demanding convergence and instead learn to manage friction between systems. The goal should be to prevent conflict between incompatible economic logics, not to eliminate the incompatibility.

- Institutionalise dialogue.

Regular communication is essential to avoid spirals of escalation. Managed trade agreements, sector-specific talks, and standing bilateral forums can act as pressure valves. Instead of crisis-driven negotiation, the US should propose enduring mechanisms to address export controls, digital standards, and subsidies. These platforms won't eliminate conflict, but they can make it more predictable and manageable.

- Invest in domestic strength.

The most effective response to external competition is internal renewal. During the Japan challenge, American resilience was powered by its own innovation surge – from Silicon Valley to biotech. The US must do the same again: invest in infrastructure, education, industrial capacity, and next-generation technologies.

- Take the long view.

Systemic rivalries are not settled in election cycles; they are measured in decades. Strategic patience is vital. That means resisting reactive policymaking and short-term theatrics in favour of building institutional, economic, and geopolitical resilience. Stability – not "victory" – is the correct metric of success.

SUMMARY TABLE: **KEY STEPS TO MANAGING THE SYSTEMS CLASH**

Step	Description
1. Set realistic objectives	Focus on narrow, achievable goals – not systemic transformation.
2. Accept systemic difference	Acknowledge China's economic model will endure; manage frictions rather than eliminate them.
3. Institutionalise dialogue	Build regular negotiation forums to manage disputes and avoid crisis escalation.
4. Invest in domestic strength	Prioritise industrial renewal, innovation, and workforce competitiveness.
5. Take the long view	Adopt a generational time horizon; measure progress in resilience, not quick wins.

The road ahead will be difficult, but not impossible. America's advantage lies not in how forcefully it challenges China, but in how wisely it adapts. In a contest between systems, the winner is not the side that breaks the other – it is the side that proves itself more stable and resilien: that's how the Cold War ended.

Summary and concluding remarks

The US–China conflict is often framed as a trade war, but mistaking a systems clash for a trade war creates dangerous expectations – and has led to the self-defeating policies of Trump's Hack. The Hack turned economic fear into policy aggression and hardened China's resolve instead of working with it. With the Chinese and their Opium War memories engraved on the national psyche, the harsher the tactics, the slimmer the prospects for pragmatic compromise.

As this chapter has shown, the core of the rivalry is not about tariffs or trade balances, but about a fundamental clash between two distinct economic systems. This clash cannot be "won" – only managed.

Neither side can force the other to abandon its model. China's state-led capitalism is a cornerstone of its political system and national identity. America's market-led system is anchored in its democratic, pluralistic institutions. The clash between these models cannot be resolved by pressure or negotiation – it can only be managed.

History provides perspective. The US–Japan conflict of the 1980s reminds us that systemic tensions can be contained, even if they cannot be resolved. But key differences – Japan's alliance with the US, its eventual economic stagnation, and its lesser integration into global supply chains – make the China case far more complex and volatile.

What's needed is not confrontation, but strategic management. This means abandoning triumphalist fantasies and adopting a sober, long-term strategy rooted in realism. It means setting limited, achievable goals. It means institutionalising dialogue. And most importantly, it means investing in America's own capacity to compete and thrive.

Closing remarks

The gravest danger in Washington's approach to China is not the tools it is using, but the assumptions behind them. By misdiagnosing a clash of systems as a conventional trade war, the US is preparing for the wrong kind of conflict. This is not a skirmish over tariffs or trade balances. It is a deep and enduring rivalry between two economic worldviews. Treating it as anything less invites the very failure policymakers hope to avoid – strategic missteps, hardened opposition, and self-inflicted harm.

In this clash of systems, the outcome will be determined by which country can adapt better, sustain domestic renewal, and project a model others wish to emulate. The true test is not how hard America can hit – but how well it can endure.

America prevailed in the Cold War, not by crushing the USSR, but by advancing US strength from within.

8   Will the Hack pull the world apart?

Scenarios for a post-American world trade order

Trump's tariffs have thrown a stone into the calm waters of the global tariff lake, creating ripples far beyond the immediate bilateral retaliations. Since his tariffs shattered decades of trust, the ripples are becoming waves. The world is rebuilding a system of global trade relations for a post-American-leadership era.

For decades, access to the US market was the bridge over troubled waters, sought after by all nations. Nations cut tariffs, signed trade deals, and adapted their commercial strategies to ensure they had access to that bridge. But now, with a stroke of the presidential pen, the" bridge over troubled waters" turned into a drawbridge.

The big question is this: How will the world respond?

When the United States, the former leader of the system, retreats behind tariff walls, other nations must rethink their trade strategies. Will they pull together, signing new free trade agreements that sidestep America? Or will they pull apart, succumbing to protectionist temptations and splintering into rival blocs?

This chapter examines the political economy dynamics unleashed by Trump's tariffs. It shows how classic forces – domino effects,[1] cascading tariffs,[2] and multilateralising regionalism[3] – are reshaping the world's trade map in real time. These forces identify how governments change tariffs in response to pressures from vested interests like exporters and import-competing firms.

The goal of the chapter is not to predict the future with false precision. Rather, it is to map out plausible scenarios, grounded in political-economic logic, that suggest where the world might be heading. Some scenarios are benign, some deeply damaging. But one thing is clear: the world is moving on, with or without the United States.

The political economy of tariff realignments

What exactly are these ripples? The technical name is "trade deflection".

When US tariffs go up, exporters to the US don't just reduce supply to match the reduction in sales to the US. They redirect their exports to other countries. Tariffs, in a sense, deflects the exports to other markets.

The redirection changes things on both the exporters' side and the side of firms in nations that experience the import surge cause by the redirection. Each side generates

1   Baldwin, R. E. (1993). A domino theory of regionalism (NBER Working Paper No. 4465). National Bureau of Economic Research. https://www.nber.org/papers/w4465
2   Irwin, D. A. (2017). *Clashing over commerce: A history of US trade policy*. University of Chicago Press.
3   Baldwin, R. E. (2006). Multilateralising regionalism: Spaghetti bowls as building blocs on the path to global free trade. The World Economy, 29(11), 1451-1518. https://doi.org/10.1111/j.1467-9701.2006.00852.x

new political economy pressures to change tariffs levels. To think through what is likely to happen to tariffs today, we need some background on what drives trade policy.

Why do countries change their tariffs?

Countries don't adjust their tariffs because they read about comparative advantage in an economics textbook. They don't lower their tariffs out of a platonic romance with free trade.

A country's tariffs are the outcome of domestic politics. Domestic political processes set tariffs at the level where the political muscle of the pro-tariff crowd just offsets the political muscle of the anti-tariff crowd.[4]

How does this apply to situations where the government is thinking about raising or lower the existing tariffs? Whether the government put them up or down, changing tariffs creates winners and losers inside the nation changing them. That, in turn, launches domestic political battles, which may be won by the pro-liberalisation political forces or by the pro-protection forces.

Note how this is different to the common way of thinking about tariff liberalisation as the outcome of international bargaining. That way of thinking is incomplete. Tariffs are the outcome of domestic political bargaining. Of course, international bargaining can affect the domestic policies, but it is the domestic process that ultimately decides whether the tariffs will be raised or lowered. The technical name for this perspective is the two-level political economy logic.[5]

The political economy mechanisms

Over the years, I have used the two-level logic to organise my thinking about tariffs changes lumping the logic into three political economy mechanisms: domino liberalisation,[6] cascading tariffs,[7] and multilateralising regionalism.[8] Together they provide a way to think systematically about the impact of Trump's Great Trade Hack on trade relations in the rest of the world.

The Domino Theory and contagious trade liberalisation

When two countries strike a free trade agreement (FTA), they create a club.

Think of it like one of those "warehouse clubs" where you pay an annual membership fee to get access to low-priced goods inside the warehouse. But with FTAs, it's not about having the right to buy inside the club, it's about having the right to sell to other

4   Grossman, G. M., & Helpman, E. (1995). Trade wars and trade talks. Journal of Political Economy, 103(4), 675-708. https://doi.org/10.1086/261999

5   Putnam, R. D. (1988). Diplomacy and domestic politics: The logic of two-level games. International Organization, 42(3), 427-460.

6   Baldwin, R. E. (1993). A domino theory of regionalism (NBER Working Paper No. 4465). National Bureau of Economic Research. https://www.nber.org/papers/w4465

7   Irwin, D. A. (2017). Clashing over commerce: A history of US trade policy. University of Chicago Press.

8   Baldwin, R. E. (2006). Multilateralising regionalism: Spaghetti bowls as building blocs on the path to global free trade. The World Economy, 29(11), 1451-1518. https://doi.org/10.1111/j.1467-9701.2006.00852.x

members' markets without paying their usual tariffs. When it comes to an FTA, the warehouse club gives you preferential tariff treatment.

Sounds like a great idea, but spare a thought for the exporters who are not in the club. They pay tariffs that their competitors inside the FTA do not. This will typically result in the excluded-nations' exporters selling less to the nations that are part of the FTA club.

This domino liberalisation logic is useful in thinking about how Trump's tariffs may induce other nations to form new free trade agreements – new warehouse clubs if you will.

Think about it. The firms that used to export to the US before 2 April 2025 are now keener on selling their goods to other markets. Lower tariffs in other markets would help them do this.

How can they secure lower tariffs in non-US markets? The best way is to get their government to sign a free trade agreement with non-US trade partners. While they surely were interested in getting lower tariffs in non-US markets even before 2 April, Trump's tariffs has made them even more interested.

The extra interest of exporters in FTAs with non-US nations gets transformed into a greater domestic political push for signing new FTAs. The extra push will not always lead to a new deal, but it will do so, and has done so, in some cases.

In short, the loss of exports to the US generates pro-FTA forces in nations around the world and the result is more trade deals among non-US countries. These, as you will have noticed, leave the US outside the newly liberated trade partnerships.

There are many historical examples of this happening. It is exactly what happened in reaction to the US 1930 Smoot-Hawley Tariff. In 1933, the UK led the Commonwealth countries into a new trade bloc called the Imperial Preference System. This granted tariff preferences to all members of the Commonwealth in all other Commonwealth economies. The preferences for the club members automatically became discrimination for non-members. The US felt the impact of the discrimination most acutely in the Canadian market.

To summarise, it's a three-step political economy mechanism. 1) When the US market closes, exporters look for alternative markets. 2) These exports lobby their own governments for new trade deals. The greater the former reliance on the US market, the more firms will be willing to spend on domestic lobbying to get deals that open alternative markets. 3) If these extra pro-FTA forces are strong enough, governments respond by negotiating new FTAs.

This domino liberalisation is already creating new clubs. Remember Trump started putting up tariffs back in 2018, and Biden removed few of them, so the rest of the world has had time to form or join free trade agreements. To name just a few:

- The long-stalled EU-Mercosur agreement was revived.[9]

- The Comprehensive and Progressive Agreement for Trans-Pacific Partnership (CPTPP) is expanding, welcoming new members like the UK.[10]

- The Indo-Pacific Economic Framework (IPEF) is deepening cooperation, even without formal market access commitments.[11]

- There is serious talk of expanding the Regional Comprehensive Economic Partnership (RCEP).[12]

These new initiatives put America on the sidelines of global trade arrangements.

Cascading protection

The second mechanism works the other way around. Whereas the domino mechanism pulls tariffs down, cascading retaliation pushes them up, so Trump's tariffs may trigger higher tariffs in the rest of the world.

Why might tariffs rise? The cascading protection mechanism starts from the same trade deflection but looks at the impact on importers rather than exporters. For example, electric vehicles (EVs) that China was selling to the US before they were hit with 100% tariffs will be sold somewhere else since the factories won't shut down. When the displaced, or "deflected", exports arrive in their markets, if these nations have domestic producers of similar goods, the import-competing companies may clamour for protection against the redirected exports.

You can see where the "cascading protection" comes from. One protectionist move sets off avalanches of retaliation that result in higher tariffs all around. In many cases, the import-competing firms can use existing trade laws, called anti-dumping laws, to get protection against the redirected exports. This is political economy mechanism is well-known and has been widely documented.[13]

Multilateralising Regionalism: Merging trade agreements

Sometimes regional trade blocs, instead of hardening into fortress walls, gradually liberalise outward. Preferential agreements can be stepping stones, not stumbling blocks.[14]

9   Sanchez Alonso, A. (2024, December 6). Von der Leyen clinches EU-Mercosur trade deal, in face of French opposition. Euronews. https://www.euronews.com/my-europe/2024/12/06/von-der-leyen-clinches-eu-mercosur-trade-deal-in-face-of-french-opposition

10 Department for Business and Trade. (2024, December 15). £2 billion boost to growth as UK joins major trade group. GOV.UK. https://www.gov.uk/government/news/2-billion-boost-to-growth-as-uk-joins-major-trade-group

11 Cimino-Isaacs, C. D., Kitamura, K. H., & Manyin, M. E. (2024, July 22). Indo-Pacific Economic Framework for Prosperity (IPEF) (CRS Report No. IF12373). Congressional Research Service. https://www.congress.gov/crs-product/IF12373

12 World Economic Forum. (2025, March 25). RCEP trade agreement and the future of multilateralism. https://www.weforum.org/stories/2025/03/rcep-how-will-this-trade-agreement-shape-multilateralism/

13 For a detailed explanation, see Irwin, D. A. (2017). *Clashing over commerce: A history of US trade policy*. University of Chicago Press. For empirical evidence, see Erbahar, A., & Zi, Y. (2017). Cascading trade protection: Evidence from the US. Journal of International Economics, 108, 274-299. https://doi.org/10.1016/j.jinteco.2017.07.007

14 Baldwin, R. E. (2006). Multilateralising regionalism: Spaghetti bowls as building blocs on the path to global free trade. The World Economy, 29(11), 1451-1518. https://doi.org/10.1111/j.1467-9701.2006.00852.x

In postwar Europe, for example, rival trade blocs – the European Economic Community (EEC) and European Free Trade Association (EFTA) – eventually integrated. The UK, feeling the domino pressure, joined the EEC in the 1970s. Industrial tariffs between Europe's two camps disappeared.[15] Competition begat cooperation.

The political economy logic is very much like the Domino Theory but operating at the level of a group of nations considering a free trade arrangement with another group of nations. Think of it like two warehouse clubs in neighbouring towns who decide to merge their membership – thereby giving better access to everyone. But now that the warehouse is so big, even more people want to join the clubs.

HOW TRUMP'S TARIFFS RESHAPE GLOBAL TRADE: THREE POLITICAL ECONOMY MECHANISMS

Mechanism	What it does	How it works	Impact on world trade
1. Domino liberalisation	Pulls tariffs down	Exporters excluded from US markets seek access elsewhere. They lobby for new free trade agreements with other countries.	More FTAs between non-US countries; US left out
2. Cascading protection	Pushes tariffs up	US tariffs deflect exports to third markets, flooding them with redirected goods. Domestic firms in those countries lobby for retaliatory protection.	A wave of tariff hikes spreads internationally
3. Multilateralising regionalism	Consolidates and expands existing trade blocs	Separate regional trade agreements merge into wider liberal networks under pressure from exporters seeking broader, cheaper access	Larger, more integrated trade zones – often excluding the US

Lessons

Trade policies change when commercial pressures overwhelm political inertia. And Trump's tariffs are dramatically reshuffling global commercial interests. Once, the US served as the central bridge connecting nations into the global trading system. Now, with the US drawbridge raised, countries are building new spans among each other. These aren't just alternative routes. They're new trade architectures taking shape without America at the centre.

15 Winters, L. A. (1996). Regionalism versus multilateralism (Policy Research Working Paper No. 1687). World Bank. http:// documents.worldbank.org/curated/en/881921468739473983

Where will all this land? Trump's tariffs unleashed powerful economic forces that are reshaping trade patterns worldwide. How these forces ultimately redraw the world trade map will depend on how governments, firms, and institutions respond.

America launched the Great Trade Hack, but the future of world trade hangs on how the rest of the world responds. The next question is: What might these forces lead to?

What next? Future scenarios for global trade

To clarify risks, highlight key turning points, and frame the urgent questions, consider four scenarios. I begin with the worst-case scenario. Not because it's likely, but because it's possible and illuminating.

A warning, not a scenario: Chaotic 1930s-style collapse

Picture this: the goods China was exporting to the US get diverted the other major manufacturing nations – the EU, India, Japan, Korea, and Britain. Their producers, suddenly facing more intense competition, demand protection. If the protection provided mimics Trump's rule-breaking, China might feel it had to retaliate, which could trigger counter-retaliation.

And the same redirection, protection, and retaliation story could raise tariffs on the imports and exports of the all the other major exporters of manufactured goods – the EU, India, Japan, and Korea, and Britain This leads to tariffs spiralling and an unravelling of trade.

But the damage might not stop there. As we saw in April, trade shocks can create financial crises. And 2009 taught us that these can trigger global recessions.

This is not a forecast – it's a thought experiment. But history provides precedent. When the US passed the Smoot-Hawley Tariff in 1930, there were no global rules to stop the ensuing retaliatory spiral. The result was a worldwide collapse in trade and the Great Depression.

Today, we have experience and institutions in place. That's why I believe full collapse is unlikely. But it is not impossible – remember how US–China retaliation pushed tariffs past 100% in just a few news cycles. Let me be clear: I'm not predicting doom. I'm highlighting how missteps could ignite a chain reaction. Forewarned is forearmed.

The most plausible three scenarios

We now turn to three other scenarios that I consider more likely. Indeed, I am pretty sure that what unfolds over the rest of 2025 will be some combination of these three. (Unless, of course, President Trump launches a new hack.)

These scenarios are grounded in a political economy framework I've used for decades. It is built on two dynamics: cascading protection and domino liberalisation. Cascades occur when trade deflection inflames protectionist pressure in third countries.

Dominoes occur when excluded exporters push their governments to open new markets through trade deals.

These forces tug in opposite directions. The three scenarios map different balances of the two.

- The first is what I call *Managed Multilateral Drift*.

The world was already on the way to this one since the dominos and cascades were launched in Trump's first term.

Regional and bilateral trade deals flourish and become the focal point of trade governance. Trade deflection is dealt with the standard, WTO-compliant tariffs which do not threaten the system. The WTO doesn't collapse, but it moves to the back of the room.

The trade blocs do not fight among themselves but neither do they coordinate in their support of rules-based multilateralism. Global trade and investment continue to grow, although perhaps only after a recession induced by Trump's Hack.

This is the messy scenario. Policies are patchier and harder to predict. But crucially, the US remains the sole systematic violator of multilateral trade norms.

Multilateralism survives but doesn't thrive.

- A darker future is the *Fighting Trade Blocs* scenario.

Here, blocs emerge – but instead of peaceful coexistence, they clash.

The most likely constellation is a three-bloc world with the US as a bloc of one (with Canada and Mexico as reluctant followers), a China-led bloc, and an EU-led bloc.

Each big manufacturing economy is in just one bloc. Other countries outside the core three try to trade with all sides, but face mounting pressure to pick a bloc.

Inter-bloc trade no longer respects most-favoured nation (MFN) norms. Trade shrinks, risk rises, and efficiency yields to geopolitics.

Multilateralism lingers but it limps.

- A third scenario is *Reglobalisation Without America*, led by "leadership herds".

I attach a low probability to this, but it isn't as unlikely as it may seem. For decades, the USSR, India, and China traded little with the world. The rest of the world carried on just fine. This scenario envisions the same happening to the United States. All the dominos fall except those involving US imports or exports.

This scenario would be built by "leadership herds". Distributed leadership coalitions composed of fluid, formless formations of large trading nations including the EU, China, Japan, Britain, Korea, India, and others. The most likely "non-leader" of these leaderless herds would be the EU. But it would be the convener and coordinator, not the leader.

Can you imagine the EU convening an informal gathering of the biggest supporters of multilateralism? No formal agenda. No group label. No exclusion. Just an exploratory conversation looking for a critical mass of like-minded trading nations interested in saving the system. I can. This is what happened when the US walked away from the Trans-Pacific Partnership (TPP) agreement. Japan organised a leader herd and got the deal done as CPTPP. It also happened when the US killed the WTO's Appellate Body and the EU organised a leadership herd to replace it with the Multi-Party Interim Appeal Arbitration Arrangement (MPIA).

In this scenario, the WTO endures. It evolves. It is no longer the anchor of the system, but rather a clearinghouse for trade-rule cooperation on 21st-century challenges like climate change, digital trade, and demographic shifts.

The WTO survives and maybe even thrives.

Here is a quick summary of the scenarios:

Scenario	Stability	Role of US	WTO status
Chaos, 1930s-style	Low	Perpetuator	Destroyed
Managed Multilateral Drift	Moderate	Marginal	Survives, diminished
Fighting Trade Blocs	Low	Defensive	Sidelined
Reglobalisation Without America	High	Minor	Possible revival

What do the realigning trade relations mean for the US?

Trump's tariffs were a stone tossed into the still waters of the global trade lake. The initial splash – higher duties, retaliation, and trade tension – was disruptive enough. But the more important impact is found in the ripples. Those ripples are spreading outward, quietly reshaping the trade strategies of America's partners.

Countries that once oriented their economies around access to the US market are now deepening ties with each other. In doing so, they are redrawing the global trade map – and leaving US exporters on the outside of new agreements, facing new disadvantages. What began as a bilateral tariff shock is evolving into a global realignment.

What do these new tariffs and new free trade agreements mean for the United States? The answer, in one word, is sobering. The reason is down to two words: trade diversion.

Trade diversion is the flip side of trade deflection. When two countries sign a free trade agreement that excludes the United States, US exporters suddenly find themselves at a competitive disadvantage – even if no new tariffs are imposed directly on them.

There is a parable that illustrates this, the "two campers and a bear story". It illustrates how it is not about being fast, but faster than the other guy.

> *"Two campers in Yellowstone National Park hear the roar of a hungry Grizzly bear just outside their tent. One camper sits up and starts putting on his running shoes. The other says: 'Are you crazy? You can't outrun a bear!' The first camper, who continues tying his laces, replies: 'Oh, I don't have to outrun the bear. I just have to outrun you.'"*

If Indonesia, for example, joins the CPTPP as it wants to do, Japanese carmakers will face lower tariffs in the Indonesia market than US-based carmakers.[16,17] In the CPTPP enlargement case, and inside the CPTPP market, US firms are like the camper without the running shoes.

This is the classic Viner logic: preferences granted to others become implicit barriers to American exporters.

Across industries like autos, agriculture, and machinery, firms that once dominated foreign markets are now being undercut by rivals who benefit from lower duties and smoother access.[18] The erosion is subtle but cumulative – each new agreement chips away at America's export competitiveness.

And it's not just about export competitiveness. The erosion of export competitiveness is matched by the erosion of American strategic leverage. The gravitational pull of the US economy weakens, not because America has shrunk, but because the rest of the world has built alternate orbits.

For decades, the promise of access to the US market gave Washington outsized influence in global trade diplomacy. But as other countries strike deals among themselves, bypassing Washington, that influence wanes. The US market becomes systematically less important to all nations in the world. That, in turn, reduces the consequences of being shut out of the American market.

China has already done this massively. Before Trump started his first trade war in 2018, China sent over 20% of its exports to the US. When Trump started his second war, that number was in the low double digits. As a consequence, the US has less leverage over China than before, and that trend will surely be accelerated by the 2 April 2025 tariffs. The US is no longer the indispensable market it once was.

In short, what began as a bid to protect American industry may end by isolating it.

16 Saputra, B., & Adji, R. (2024, September 25). Indonesia officially applies for CPTPP membership to drive exports. ANTARA News. https://en.antaranews.com/news/327247/indonesia-officially-applies-for-cptpp-membership-to-drive-exports
17 Mahardika, A., & Nugroho, P. (2025, March 8). Indonesia's ambiguous future on economic diplomacy: BRICS, OECD, or CPTPP? Modern Diplomacy. https://moderndiplomacy.eu/2025/03/08/indonesias-ambiguous-future-on-economic-diplomacy-brics-oecd-or-cptpp/
18 Viner, J. (1950). The customs union issue. New York: Carnegie Endowment for International Peace.

Conclusion: Lost markets and lost leverage

The emotional logic behind Trump's Hack – namely, the Grievance Doctrine – was silent on the future shape of the world trade system. It pulled America out of the old system, so it could use raw power to achieve its goals.

But in trade wars, as in real wars, the first casualty is control. Trump's trade war didn't just disrupt commerce. It unleashed powerful political economy forces – domino liberalisation and cascading protection – that are now reshaping the world trade map.

Over time, trade diversion reshapes the world economy. New distribution channels are built. New supply relationships are formed. Factories, contracts, and investments follow the new flows. Once trade routes shift, they tend to stay shifted.

And this erosion of competitiveness isn't just commercial. It's geopolitical. The longer the US keeps its drawbridge up, the more likely it is that the traffic it used to attract finds other bridges. This matters for America's influence in the trade system. America's leverage in the global economy has never come from tariffs – it came from centrality. For decades, the promise of access to the US market gave Washington influence over how trade rules were written and enforced. That influence is fading. A market that once acted as a magnet for global exporters is now seen as unpredictable, volatile, and politically weaponised. That weakens America's hand.

Trump's tariffs have set in motion a slow but significant realignment of the world's trade architecture – one where the US is no longer the central pillar, but just another player.

Think of it this way. Trump threw the stone into the lake without thinking about all the consequences. But ripples have a way of becoming waves. And the waves are now rising.

When the waves finally break, America may find the world has already learned to trade without it.

9 Did the Hack break the world trade order?

When the systems administrator turned hacker

President Trump's Great Trade Hack, the April 2nd tariffs, shattered more than just trade flows. They shattered trust in US leadership of the world trade system.

America was the architect of the postwar multilateral order. Through vision, leadership, and enormous economic weight, it built the system that tied prosperity to predictability thorough a simple set of rules that everyone played by.

This was enlightened self-interest, not an act of charity. America's economy thrived. For instance, while the other G7 nations have seen their shares of world GDP decline as China's rose, the US held its own. Its share of global GDP was about a quarter in 1995, and it is still a quarter now. The enlightened self-interest also bolstered American power in areas ranging from the Cold War to the War on Terror.

Because American leadership served US interests so well, the world assumed that no matter how turbulent US politics became, Washington would remain the systems administrator.

With a single presidential signature, Donald Trump disproved their assumption. On 2 April 2025. the systems administrator started hacking the system.

Trump's Hack hit more than just trade flows and global trust – it directly assaulted the very idea of a rules-based system.

While Trump never articulated a vision for the system's future, his actions suggest a belief that there should be no system at all. He wants a "non-system system", so to speak. He wants the law of the jungle to overtake the law of international trade.

The key question the world faces now is: Did Trump's Hack corrupt the source code of the multilateral trade system?

This chapter tackles that question by breaking it into three sub-questions:

- How did Trump's Hack threaten the world trade system?

- Is America's leadership abdication temporary or permanent?

- Who will be the next systems administrator?

How did Trump's Hack threaten the world trade system?

Trump's Hack targeted the very idea that global trade should be governed by rules rather than raw power. This threatened the heart of the system.

How so? In fact, no one country or body is in charge of enforcing the WTO rules. The rules are followed, and therefore they work, because members believe all members will follow them. Trust in the system is the system.

The Hack's two "attack vectors"

When the world's largest importer, and long-standing champion of the rules, turned rule-breaker on 2 April, the system was imperilled. The real threat is that rule-breaking could become contagious. If the country that built the system, and benefited heavily from it, now openly disregards its rules, why should others continue to comply?

To dig deeper, consider the two foundational WTO principles Trump disregarded: non-discrimination and promise-keeping (tariff "bindings").

- Systemic violation of WTO's non-discrimination principle.

The WTO rests on a few simple principles. Chief among them is non-discrimination. For historical reasons, non-discrimination is called most-favoured nation (MFN). It is not a sidebar or after thought. It is literally Article 1 of the WTO rulebook.[1]

In plain terms, MFN means if you lower a trade barrier for one country, you lower it for every WTO member. No favourites allowed, except in carefully curated cases like free trade agreements and retaliation against unfair trade policies.

This principle, championed by America for eighty years, underpinned the global economy, benefiting American firms by ensuring a level playing field.

Why was MFN embraced for so long? The MFN principle offers a mix of practical efficiency and political fairness that has helped sustain the global trading system for decades. It allows tariff liberalisation to advance at each country's own pace while automatically extending the benefits to all WTO members. This was a practical side of MFN. It eliminated the need for negotiating with all the WTO members every time any tariff changed with anybody.

There is also another very practical side to MFN. It reduces the need to prove the origin of imports since imports from everywhere pay the same tariff (free trade partners are an exception). Consider the complexity it avoids. The US applies tariffs on approximately 15,000 distinct products, and it imports from almost 200 different territories. With MFN, there is no incentive to misrepresent the origin of a product, so customs officials can be rather relaxed about origin. With Trump's system, by contrast, customs must verify whether imports, such as Chinese socks, are genuinely from China or transhipped through Singapore to dodge higher tariffs. Each product line needs its own rule, multiplying red tape exponentially.

1   World Trade Organization. (n.d.). Principles of the trading system: Trade without discrimination. Retrieved from https://www.wto.org/english/thewto_e/whatis_e/tif_e/fact2_e.htm

Also, by limiting favouritism, MFN shields weaker nations from political pressure by larger powers demanding special treatment, reinforcing the neutrality of the system. Crucially, it gives smaller trading nations a meaningful stake in the rules. Indeed, the promise of MFN treatment is a powerful incentive to join the WTO and to play by its rules once you're in. In this way, MFN has been a quiet force for cohesion, helping to hold the trade system together even as the political and economic landscape has shifted dramatically.

All this goes to say that Trump's rejection of MFN is not a small thing. His "reciprocity" April 2nd tariffs were a direct attack on MFN, which was, due to the principle's centrality, an attack on the whole system.

- Systematic reneging on US tariff bindings.

Trump's second systemic violation involved disregarding America's tariff commitments made since 1947. These commitments, called "tariff bindings", were the bedrock of predictable global trade – assuring businesses tariffs wouldn't arbitrarily rise after investments were made.

Historically, tariff bindings emerged from multilateral negotiations under the General Agreement on Tariffs and Trade (GATT), which became the WTO in 1995. America spearheaded these negotiations, leveraging its market size to shape rules and lower barriers globally.

Reciprocity in these rounds was about mutual benefit: "I'll lower some of mine if you lower some of yours". Crucially, reciprocity didn't mean matching goods for goods, but rather exchanging tariff reductions of comparable commercial significance – such as Japanese wheat tariffs being lowered in exchange for US car tariffs.

The third way the Unites States has undermine the rules-based system is by killing its court.

Death of the WTO's dispute settlement system

Trump's fingerprints are not the only ones on the knife that slayed the WTO's dispute settlement system. Obama's and Biden's are on the knife handle as well. Yet Trump's historically disruptive April 2nd tariffs delivered the final coup.

This matters. Trade rules work best when all members can turn to a neutral party to adjudicate disputes. Think of it as the trusted committee of a neighbourhood association that settles local disputes. The committee's judgements don't make everyone happy, but they help keep a lid on frictions. If the committee were disbanded, neighbours would start handling things themselves, and calm could give way to endless feuds.

Since 1995, the WTO's dispute settlement mechanism has been the world's trusted committee.[2] It died in 2019 when America's blocking of appointments led to the situation where there were not enough judges to hear even a single case.[3] It was a strategic move on the part of the first Trump administration. Without a functioning court, the US could violate trade rules without fear of losing before the court. For a trade system built on rules, this was dynamite thrown into the foundation.

What would death of the rules-based system look like?

The death of the rules-based system will, I believe, come the way F. Scott Fitzgerald – channelling T.S. Eliot – might have imagined it. Not with a bang, but a long unwinding – slowly at first, then all at once.

Trust, you see, is like a social norm. People abide by it because they believe others will, too. But once some start breaking the norm, others begin to question whether they should keep following it. Such doubt is reflective, and contagious. As more actors doubt, hesitate, and violate, the social norm unravels at an accelerating pace.

The end result would not, in my view, be a world without rules. It would be a bit like the traffic in a congested emerging market city. Even if everyone knows the official rules of the road, no one dares follow them since no one else is. What emerges is chaotic negotiation at every intersection, and an embrace of dog-eat-dog ethos. The result is confusion, inefficiency, and rising cost for all.

In the trade world, the equivalent would be nations falling back on tactical, transactional behaviour and a "might makes right" world. If that came to pass, things would be bad. Would it be too provocative to suggest that the WTO building might be turned into a museum to show young people what it was like to live in a prosperous, cooperative world?

The irony of such an outcome would be rich.

When it was the undisputed leader, the United States was the rule maker; other WTO members were rule takers. The US had long relied on the rules-based order to amplify its influence and constrain its rivals. But having set fire to the rulebook, America will find itself more isolated, less persuasive, and with just one diplomatic tool left: threats to close its market even more. In short, breaking the system may also have broken one of its greatest sources of worldwide influence.

2   World Trade Organization. (n.d.). Understanding the WTO: Settling disputes-A unique contribution. Retrieved from https://www.wto.org/english/thewto_e/whatis_e/tif_e/disp1_e.htm

3   Lester, S. (2022, March 2). Ending the WTO dispute settlement crisis: Where to from here? International Institute for Sustainable Development. https://www.iisd.org/articles/united-states-must-propose-solutions-end-wto-dispute-settlement-crisis

Conclusion: Trump's legacy - the end of American trade leadership

Trump's tariffs started as a unilateral assault on imports but ended up – intentionally or not – as a unilateral abdication of leadership. When the United States switched from system administrator to system hacker, the world's universal recognition of American stewardship turned into universal suspicion of America.

The April 2nd tariffs dealt a direct blow to the WTO system. For the first time, the world's largest importer purposefully and forcefully violated core WTO rules. The survival of rules-based trade is menaced by these violations. Is the source code compromised? Is the system collapsing?

So far, so good. The damage remains contained. It is early days, but we have not seen any hints of America's wilful disregard of the rule spreading beyond Washington. Even more encouraging is the way the vacuum created by America's withdrawal is starting to be filled. New forms of leadership seem to be emerging or at least gestating.

That's the hopeful part. The most likely future is not the collapse of multilateralism, but a messier version of it.

The future is always uncertain, but this part of it is not. If the WTO survives, it will no longer revolve around Washington.

America built the system, ran the system, then hacked the system. The world is rebooting the system and moving on.

10 Strategies for the post-American-leadership era

To defend the rules-based system, follow the rules and cooperate with "leadership herds"

Trump's April 2nd tariffs were an assault on the exports of every trade partner. They were also an assault on the world trade system.

As Chapter 8 argued, Trump's Great Trade Hack was a brazen, deliberate rule-breaking by the world's largest importer and the country the world used to see as the leader of multilateralism. With one stroke of the pen, the US abandoned two of the system's foundational principles – non-discrimination and promise keeping – and made clear that it would no longer be constrained by multilateral discipline.

If Chapter 8 was about a systems administrator corrupting the operating code, this chapter is about what the rest of the crew does when the captain jumps ship (after having set fire to the navigation charts).

This is the new reality. A reality that the rest of the world must deal with since this is not a case of the captain going temporarily insane. As Chapter 2 argued, the bipartisan consensus in Washington is now trade hesitant at best. The US has abandoned its captaincy of the multilateral trade ship and it's not coming back anytime soon. We are, in short, in the post-American leadership era.

The question now is: How does the crew – the rest of the world – keep the ship upright and on course without its captain?

Point one is just common sense. If the captain has jumped ship, the worst thing the crew can do is start fighting among themselves. Trump's tariffs have already thrown grit into the gears of the global trade machine – raising costs, disrupting supply chains, and undermining trust. But the damage could get exponentially worse if other countries respond in kind. If each nation reacts with its own brand of economic nationalism, tit-for-tat, and trade aggression, we risk triggering a downward spiral – one that could take us back to the 1930s, when a wave of retaliatory tariffs helped turn a financial crisis into a global depression.

The threat today is not just what Washington has done, but what others may now feel compelled to do – against the US and against each other. If leaders act out of anger, panic, or pride, the world trade system may fracture beyond repair. Restraint is not weakness, it's wisdom.

The Prime Directive: Defend the rules by following them

The Prime Directive, to pull up a Star Trek meme, is simple: defend the rules-based trade system by following the rules.

Retaliation, if undertaken, must be disciplined – precise, proportionate, and explicitly grounded in WTO rules. When countermeasures are legally justified, publicly explained, and clearly framed as rule-consistent, they send the right signal – that the system is still functioning, that principles still matter. The goal is not to mimic US behaviour but to outlast it. Retaliation outside the rules would only confirm Trump's view that the rules no longer apply. The higher ground here is also the strongest ground. In short: fight the chaos but do it with the rulebook in hand.

But nations can do more to defend the system.

Three strategic choices: Wait, defend, or act

Beyond following the Prime Directive, the rest of the world faces three strategic choices. Three strategic pathways suggest themselves: wait, defend, or act.

Strategic patience (wait & see)

As of May 2025, when this book went to print, the wisest move for most countries is to wait. The immediate goal should be to avoid self-inflicted damage. That means holding steady, watching how things unfold inside the US, and avoiding all provocations of Uncle Sam. A week after imposing them, Trump suspended his April 2nd tariffs for 90 days.

There are good reasons to think Trump's tariffs might not never get reimposed. He suspended them to stop a market turmoil so severe that he feared it might lead to another Global Financial Crisis. That danger still exists.

One way to think about Trump's position is to picture a tough guy trying to hold his arm over a candle for 90 days. My bet is that the heat – domestic pressure from businesses, consumers, and markets – will prove unbearable. Sooner or later, he'll jerk his arm away, announcing "deals" that provide the fig leaf he needs to back down with dignity.

I see two big reasons Trump will back down: pain on Main Street, and pain on Wall Street.

• Pain on Main Street.

It's clear from what happened in April that the president did not fully understand the consequences of his Hack. The most extreme measure – a 145% tariff on Chinese goods – triggered an immediate, massive drop in shipments to the US of Chinese final goods and industrial parts and components.

Since container ships take about a month to arrive on the US West Coast, the real damage is just beginning to hit in May. It is like China imposed a wartime embargo on US manufacturing, except it was Trump imposing the embargo on America, not the Chinese.

As summer progresses, US factories that rely on Chinese inputs will start to slow down, shut down, and lay off workers. Replacement suppliers can't be found fast enough.

At the same time, American consumers are already seeing higher prices. The Barbie dolls and lawn chairs missing from Walmart will most definitely be noticed by American voters.

And these product-level problems are matched by economy-wide problems. The US economy is already wobbling: one quarter of negative growth, with signs that a recession may be looming.

As the pain spreads across the US middle class, Trump will become increasingly desperate to cut deals that let him back down without looking weak. That means symbolic agreements with trade partners, even if the substance is thin.

- Pain on Wall Street.

The 2 April 2025 tariffs nearly triggered a second Global Financial Crisis. On 9 April, President Trump abruptly suspended most of the tariffs for 90 days. When asked by reporters if it was because of the market meltdown, he said: "They were getting yippy, you know, they were getting a little bit yippy, a little bit afraid." Yippy, in the world of golf, means losing your nerve under pressure (I looked it up).

Markets were already rattled by a trifecta of risk: Trump's $4.5 trillion tax cut plan, reckless cuts to public spending by an unelected enforcer, and open attacks on the judiciary. The tariffs tipped sentiment over the edge. As one analyst put it, the tariffs were "the straw that broke the camel's back – but, in defence of the camel, it was a really big straw".

On 8 and 9 April it looked, momentarily, like the start of a financial meltdown schoolchildren might someday study as the "Trump Economic Crisis of 2025".

The policy retreat was as disordered as the initial tariffs. Trump announced the suspension via social media while his trade representative, Jaime Greer, was defending the tariffs before Congress. Greer found out via a phone notification – at the witness table, live on camera.

Trump later explained the decision had been drafted "from the heart", without lawyers, in a late-night scramble with advisors Bessant and Lutnick, veterans of the 2008 crisis. But the markets remain wary. The threat of large, endless US fiscal deficits and an administration that seems cavalier about generating massive uncertainty are keeping markets primed for collapse. Markets put the safety back on their big guns, but they haven't put them back in the arms locker. The crisis is paused, not resolved.

- The domestic pain is undermining Trump's negotiating leverage.

When one side of a negotiation is in a rush to get a deal, the other side should leverage the rush to get a better deal.

Wise governments will wait until Trump is most eager to retreat – then negotiate from strength. The first such deal – the UK–US agreement announced on 8 May 2025 – suggested that Trump was already in a hurry in early May.

President Trump and UK Prime Minister Keir Starmer announced the "deal" to reduce trade tensions. But it wasn't a formal agreement; it was a hastily released White House factsheet and a UK press release. The details were sparse. The urgency was clear. Reports suggest Trump made an unexpected, late-night call to the British prime minister to seal the deal. The result was more symbol than substance – but symbol was exactly what Trump needed.

Other nations should learn the lessons. Resist rising to Trumpian provocation, waiting for pressure to mount, doing the deal, and then pretending it's a trade agreement even if it's just a press release.

In short, don't rush. Let the pain build. Then do the deal. And when you do, let the president say he won. This is how he caves in to pressure while spinning it as a genius-level play.

My incautious conjecture is that Trump will back down permanently before the 90 days are up. Where will the tariffs land? I'd guess he'll reset them to 10% on all, with a 50% add-on for imports from China and maybe a little something for the EU. That is what he promised on the campaign trail.

The next set of policies should, in my view, be embraced by all nations, regardless of whether they retaliate against the US.

Rules-based defence (guarding the 85%)
US actions have directly torn up the rules for about 15% of world trade (America's share) but need not mess up the rules for the other 85% of world trade. Above all, WTO members must avoid falling into the trap of acting as unilaterally and recklessly as the Trump administration has.

The WTO rulebook remains flexible enough to allow countries to take defensive measures – including retaliating against the United States – while still respecting multilateral rules. Reacting within the rulebook is an essential part of guarding the system. The point is not simply to defend narrow national interests, but to show that US disruption has not triggered a wholesale abandonment of the principles that have underpinned global trade, investment, and prosperity for the past 80 years.

One important strategy is to file legal complaints at the WTO. Even if enforcement is weak, the rulings provide clarity – publicly demonstrating how US actions violate agreed rules and why countermeasures are justified. As discussed in the previous chapter, US tariffs may also lead to trade deflection – a surge of displaced goods into third-country markets – which can legally justify anti-dumping or safeguard measures under WTO rules. But here, discipline matters. New tariffs must be the result of a deliberative process, carefully calibrated and limited to particular products and partners. In loudly announcing that their defensive measures are WTO-consistent and in direct response to US WTO-inconsistent actions, other nations can underline the importance of rules and avoid the appearance that the world trading system is sliding into a "might-makes-right" regime.

But holding the line isn't enough. The system could also evolve to withstand future shocks.

Proactive multilateralism (adapt and reinforce)

Beyond defence, adaptation is important. The global trading system remains robust – 85% of world trade occurs outside US borders. To preserve it, countries should deepen regional and inter-regional agreements. And, as discussed in the last chapter, I believe the forces of domino liberalisation will lead them to do so.

Initiatives like EU–Mercosur, RCEP expansion, and CPTPP enlargement are not just about economic opportunity. They are about building structural resilience. By weaving denser, rules-based networks, economies can maintain open trade even if US disruptions persist.

Finally, nations should reinforce the institutions that still work. Strengthening the Multi-Party Interim Appeal Arbitration Arrangement (MPIA) is vital. While imperfect, the MPIA keeps the principle of two-stage dispute settlement alive within the WTO framework. Expanding its membership, improving its efficiency, and building its credibility would show that even if the United States walks away from multilateralism, the rest of the world will not.

The objective, ultimately, is clear: defend the system where possible, adapt where necessary, and demonstrate, by example, that rules-based trade can survive and thrive without Washington's leadership.

To recap, the rest of the world should obey the Prime Directive: guard the rules-based system by following the rules. That is how the crew keeps the ship intact without a captain. It is how we prevent global trade from collapsing into a 1930s-style spiral of rising tariffs and falling cooperation.

But who fills the leadership vacuum?

Reclaiming global trade leadership

As Chapter 9 showed, America stepped down for global trade leadership almost twenty years ago, and it will not step back up any time soon. Given America's indefinite absence from trade leadership, alternative structures must emerge.

Who takes the reins? Alternative centres of global trade leadership

The vacuum left by America's retreat is being filled. The rest of the world is not standing still. Some are manoeuvring quietly to fill the leadership gap.

- Could the European Union be the leader?

The first and most obvious candidate is Europe. The European Union has long seen itself as a "normative power" – an entity that shapes the world not through military force but through rules, standards, and economic influence. In the trade domain, Brussels has moved decisively since Trump's first term. While Washington was busy tearing down bridges, Europe was busy building new ones – striking free trade deals with Japan, Mercosur, Vietnam, and now courting Southeast Asia and Africa. The EU's Carbon Border Adjustment Mechanism (CBAM) and digital services regulations are already setting de facto global standards. Europe may not have the military muscle of the United States, but it has market power – and it is learning how to use it to shape global rules.

Yet Europe's leadership comes with limits. The EU is a regulatory superpower, not a geopolitical one. Its internal divisions, especially over China and security issues, make it a less-than-perfect heir to the US role. Europe can lead on setting norms, but it cannot, alone, guarantee the stability of the system.

While Europe's leadership would be based on norms, Chinese leadership would, if it emerges, lead with its network centrality.

- Could the China be the leader?

The second contender is China. In terms of trade volumes, China is already at the centre of many global supply chains. Its Belt and Road Initiative, its leadership in RCEP, and its application to join the CPTPP all show that Beijing understands the power of shaping trade networks. But China faces its own contradictions. It is deeply invested in the global trading system, but wary of taking on the burdens of leadership. Moreover, many countries – especially India and countries in Europe and Southeast Asia – are reluctant to accept Chinese leadership without reservation.

Because its manufacturing superpower status appeared so rapidly, almost every major WTO member has some trade beef with China – even if not all of them have made formal complaints. Moreover, China's blend of state capitalism and political authoritarianism makes it a complicated champion for a rules-based system.

Given the difficulty of a single power taking over from the US, we must consider alternatives. Leadership tomorrow may look very different from the past, where one nation held the reins.

From hegemon to herd: Collective leadership by coalition

The world trade order is, I believe, heading to a looser, more informal pattern of leadership. One where pragmatic coalitions of the willing step up when needed. Think of it as a "leadership herd" rather than traditional leadership. No titles. No G-this or G-that. No institutions.

The leadership herd idea

The seeds of such coalition-led leadership already exist. We have two recent examples of leadership herds working. After all, April 2025 was not the first time the US shirked its leadership role at the WTO.

- Europe's dress rehearsal for a post-American-leadership era

When the US effectively killed the WTO's Appellate Body in the late 2010s by refusing to approve new judges, it walked away from the responsibility of enforcing the very rules it once championed.

Other members, led by the EU, saw a leadership vacuum and decided to fill it. But not in the usual way. It took a formless form as they worked quietly, with a whole convoy of WTO members, to set up a replacement. The way they did this holds important lessons for the future of world trade leadership.

Launched in 2020, the MPIA provided a substitute appeals process for WTO disputes among participating members. Using a little-known provision of WTO law – Article 25 of the Dispute Settlement Understanding – it allowed countries to opt into an arbitration mechanism that mirrored the structure and principles of the now-defunct Appellate Body. This legal creativity ensured that trade rulings remained subject to appeal and that disputes didn't spiral into ungovernable tit-for-tat escalation. In a sense, the MPIA kept the lights on in the WTO legal order for those who still believed in it.

The EU advanced the initiative under the steady hand of Phil Hogan, then the EU Trade Commissioner – effectively Europe's trade minister. Though he held no formal position in the global trade system, Hogan led without a title, forging and steering a diverse coalition of over 20 WTO members – including, notably, China.

A second example is how Japan guided the revival of the TPP into the CPTPP after the first Trump administration declared it "dead on arrival".

- Japan's leadership herd saves TPP

Japan organised a leadership herd to save the TPP from US withdrawal. It acted as a quiet engineer, patiently building pragmatic frameworks to keep the cooperation alive as the great powers clashed. The tale bears retelling. After Trump abruptly pulled out of the original Trans-Pacific Partnership in 2017, many thought it dead. Instead, Japan surprised the world. Working methodically behind the scenes, Tokyo led the effort to salvage the agreement.

The result was the Comprehensive and Progressive Agreement for Trans-Pacific Partnership – an ambitious, high-standard trade pact linking economies across Asia, Oceania, and the Americas. It is now growing. The UK joined and others are thinking about it. This was a classic example of a leadership herd pushing ahead after American leadership evaporated.

- Will the creation of the MPIA and CPTPP serve as templates for the post-American-leadership era?

These examples suggest that a nucleus of committed members can step up, plug holes, and keep the system functional. It points to a future of pragmatic, plurilateral, principle-driven governance.

Hooking back to the captain-less ship metaphor: in a world without a flagship, it's better to sail in convoy than try to go it alone.

The key is cooperation, flexibility, and mutual interests

The key to making the leadership herd approach work is coordination across coalitions.

No single group – whether CPTPP, RCEP, or the EU – is broad enough or strong enough to anchor the system alone. But taken together, they represent a critical mass of the world economy. If these groups can build common positions on key issues – such as digital trade rules, environmental standards, and dispute settlement procedures – they can provide stability, predictability, and even innovation at the global level.

Of course, coalitions are messy. They lack the discipline that comes from a dominant leader. Interests will diverge, priorities will clash, and enforcement will be patchy. But in the absence of American leadership, messy coalitions are better than no leadership at all.

This is where leadership herds come in. As we saw when the system overcame American moves against the Appellate Body and against TPP, the goal is not to replicate the centralised, hegemonic order of the late 20th century. That era is over. The goal now is to weave a flexible, resilient network of agreements and alliances that can defend the core principles of open trade even as geopolitical competition heats up.

Conclusion: Navigating the post-American trade system

The era of uncontested US trade leadership is over – and it's not coming back. Under Trump, America didn't just abandon the helm – it jumped overboard and threw the compass in the sea. The world must now learn to navigate without its former captain.

The challenge is urgent but clear. The rules-based trading system – long the keel of global prosperity – is under strain. Letting it splinter would destabilise more than trade; it would undermine the predictability modern economies depend on. The world must hold the ship steady. And to do that, it must, first and foremost, follow the Prime Directive:

- Save the rules-based system by following the rules.

That means resisting the urge to fight chaos with more chaos. Retaliation against US violations must be disciplined – legal, proportionate, and transparent. Rule-consistent responses don't just defend national interests – they signal that multilateralism still works, even if the United States no longer leads it. The higher ground here is also the strongest.

But the Prime Directive alone is not enough. The Prime Directive offers the behavioural compass for each nation. To chart the ship's course, we need leadership herds.

Without a single leader at the helm, the system will only endure if others step forward – together. This is where leadership herds come in: informal, flexible coalitions that act when needed, without titles or top-down command. As the EU's quiet creation of the MPIA and Japan's rescue of the TPP showed, determined clusters of countries can plug holes, patch sails, and keep the vessel moving.

This won't be a grand victory. There will be no dramatic conquest over American protectionism. The best we can hope for is to contain the damage Trump's Hack is causing, while waiting to see if the harm to America will lead its president to step back. In this new era, progress will come not from heroic speeches or sweeping treaties, but from quiet coordination, pragmatic rulemaking, and the refusal to let the system drift into irrelevance.

If the past century taught us anything, it's that global trade flourishes not when might makes right, but when rules make markets. That truth matters more than ever now.

The trading system won't be saved by waiting for America to return. It will be saved because others refused to let it sink. Not by captains, but by coalitions of the caring. Not by loud declaration, but by quiet stubbornness.

And if this works – if the system survives – it will feel like diligence, not triumph.

11   Why leaders must step up

Save the system to save global prosperity

The global trade system – indeed, global prosperity itself – is under threat.

In April 2025, the world's largest economy firebombed that system with waves of incendiary tariffs. What happens next will determine whether the system burns or rebuilds.

The greatest danger isn't what the United States has done. It's what the rest of the world might do next.

If other countries follow Washington's recklessness, the whole system could ignite. Tariff vigilantism could replace rules-based cooperation, and trust would collapse – and with it, the institutions and norms that have sustained global prosperity for generations. That outcome is not inevitable. For the moment it doesn't seem likely. But it is imaginable. It shows just how much is at stake.

If, instead, other countries defend the rules-based system by following the rules, disaster can be avoided. Global prosperity can be guarded. The system can rebuild.

This is why leaders must step up now. Not to counter Trump's Great Trade Hack but to prevent, through their own actions, the fire from engulfing the world economy.

From chaos to clarity – what Trump's tariffs really meant

The April 2025 tariffs were driven by a sense of victimhood and grievance – what I call the Grievance Doctrine. Imposing the tariffs was not a means to an end. It was the end. The act itself was visible, aggressive, and emotionally satisfying to a political base convinced that America had been cheated and humiliated.

The tariffs were about revenge – revenge against China, against globalist elites, and revenge against a system that, according to the Grievance Doctrine, was rigged against the American middle class.

That's why the April 2nd tariffs were emotionally coherent, but economically incoherent. And it's why they will not achieve their stated goals.

As shown in earlier chapters, tariffs cannot help the middle class, most of whom work in service sectors untouched by Trump's measures. They cannot reindustrialise America since that would require things that tariffs don't provide. Things like sustained, long-term investments, restored infrastructure, and trained workers.

Nor can tariffs fix the US trade deficit, which stems from an economy-wide imbalance: the fact that America spends more than it produces. In a full-employment economy, tariffs cannot raise economy-wide production or reduce aggregate demand. Unless, that is, the tariffs induce a recession, and even then, the fix is only temporary.

But America's protectionism is not temporary. As Chapter 4 showed, the shift from trade hesitancy to trade hostility didn't begin with Trump, and it won't end with him. What Trump did was normalise protectionism, turning it from the exception to the default setting.

Ironically, US tariffs will persist not despite their economic ineffectiveness, but because of it. American protectionism operates like a looping GIF: middle-class malaise creates pressure to act, real solutions are politically toxic, so politicians use tariffs to deflect blame. When tariffs fail to deliver relief, the malaise persists – and the cycle repeats.

Leaders must understand this cycle if they are to craft a savvy response to Trump's Hack.

American grievance drives the tariffs, and the goals attached to them. But because those goals are unachievable, world leaders should ignore what Trump says he wants and focus on what the politics of grievance actually demand. Above all, they should not confuse the Grievance Doctrine for a strategic plan. The US political system is now more interested in optics than outcomes.

Worse yet, if other leaders follow Trump's lead and allow their own trade policies to be shaped by vengeance, the global trading system won't just erode. It could collapse.

What next? Four future scenarios for global trade

Global trade has come to a roundabout with many exits. Chapter 8 explored four. Each scenario looks ahead to what might come next – and how that future depends on how the rest of the world responds to America's retreat.

The first is unlikely but not impossible. It's *"Chaos, 1930s-style"* – a free fall into rule-breaking, retaliation, and trade anarchy. Without credible leadership or enforcement, countries impose tariffs for domestic showmanship and strategic coercion. Norms disintegrate. The WTO becomes irrelevant. Trust and cooperation evaporate. Everyone loses.

The second is *"Managed Multilateral Drift"*. Here there is no collapse and the US remains the sole rule-breaker, but there is little coherence.

The world is already drifting in this direction, a trend shaped by what Chapter 8 called "domino liberalisation" and "cascading protection" – patterns already triggered by Trump's first-term tariffs. In this future, regional and bilateral trade deals dominate. Trade deflected from America is redirected through WTO-compliant channels that raise tariffs without raising doubts about respect for the rules.

The WTO fades but does not fall. Trade blocs co-exist without open conflict, yet they fail to coordinate in defence of multilateralism. Global trade and investment continue but the landscape becomes patchier and harder to navigate. This is the messy middle: multilateralism survives but does not thrive.

The third is *"Fighting Trade Blocs"*. Trade blocs harden along geopolitical lines. The US, EU, China, India, and regional alliances build exclusive spheres of influence and erect tariffs against each other. Smaller nations are pressured into picking a bloc. Trade continues, but trust collapses. Efficiency gives way to redundancy. Global cooperation on broader issues like climate change dies a slow death.

The fourth is *"Reglobalisation Without America."* In this scenario, America faces high tariffs on its imports and exports and continues to ignore WTO rules. The rest of the world carries on and defends the existing trade order.

Though low probability, it's hardly unthinkable. The global economy operated for decades without the USSR, India, or China. Here, the United States isolates itself while the rest of the world liberalises. In the extreme case, all the dominos fall – except those involving US trade.

A key element here is what I call "leadership herds". These are formless, loosely coordinated coalitions – comprising the EU, China, Japan, Britain, Korea, India, and others. Different herds form to address different challenges. In fact, we've already seen two successful examples: Japan assembled a leadership herd to salvage the TPP after US withdrawal, and the EU did the same to create the MPIA after Washington paralyzed the WTO's Appellate Body.

In this scenario, the WTO doesn't collapse – it evolves. No longer the system's anchor, the WTO adapts to be a clearinghouse for cooperation, and a facilitator of rule-writing on climate, digital trade, and demographic change. The rules-based system survives – and maybe even thrives.

Here is a quick summary of the scenarios:

Scenario	Trade	WTO status
Chaos, 1930s-style	Collapses	Destroyed
Managed Multilateral Drift	Grows	Survives, diminished
Fighting Trade Blocs	Grows slowly	Sidelined
Reglobalisation Without America	Grows well	Possible revival

How the rest of the world should respond

The Great Trade Hack was an American earthquake – but the aftershocks are global. Trump's April 2025 tariffs shattered assumptions, rewrote norms, and injected volatility into the world economy. But they also clarified the stakes.

The choices made in the next few months – by leaders in Brussels, Beijing, Tokyo, Delhi, and beyond – will shape the future of global prosperity for decades. What should they do?

- First: wait and see where President Trump's tariffs land.

We should know much more by July 2025. My incautious guess, based on campaign rhetoric and early announcements, is a baseline of 10% on all imports, with additional penalties on Chinese goods. Perhaps the EU will face a similar add-on.

Given the arrangements Trump reached by mid-May with the UK, leaders should abandon any hope that tariffs will return to pre-April 2nd levels in the foreseeable future. Even if Trump leaves office, the structural drivers – grievance politics and middle-class insecurity – will persist. And protectionism will persist with them.

- Second, and this is the most important point: protect the rules-based system by following the rules.

WTO rules allow lots of ways to retaliate and liberalise. Using WTO-consistent anti-dumping actions and using the dispute settlement system can avoid spiralling retaliation and establish legal clarity.

- The third point is: negotiate, don't retaliate.

Only China and the EU are big enough to stand up to the arm-twister America has become. Their willingness to do so is a service to the world. Someone has to stand up to bullies.

- The fourth point is: choose patience over provocation.

Leave the door to the US open. Trump's Great Trade Hack defines the present, but it need not define the future.

Just as most Brits have come to regret Brexit and the country is feeling its way to closer EU relations, it is entirely possible that Trump's Hack creates a backlash against the backlash. A roaring recession and intensifying inflation could change a lot of minds about the usefulness of tariffs as a solution to middle-class malaise.

That's why global leaders should keep it polite. Keep it diplomatic, and signal openness to re-engage if American political winds shift. Global prosperity is strongest when the US is inside the house. Best then, to not lock the door.

- The fifth point is: this Hack may have a silver lining.

To date, the WTO has been unable to make the rules needed to prepare the trade system for the 21st-century challenges – climate change, digitalisation, and AI-driven disruption. Maybe a new "leadership herd" could start work on those. The leadership herd could do more than protect the system – they could advance it.

For this to work, the very idea of leadership must be redefined. Leadership tomorrow will not be about dominance. It will be about coordination, persistence, and mutual interests. In the post-American leadership era, power lies not in imposing rules but in convening coalitions. The era of hegemonic liberalism is over. The era of collaborative liberalism must begin.

Leaders must step up now; the future won't wait

This book traces a sobering reality while pointing to a hopeful path forward.

Since US protectionism is structural, and tariffs won't fix America's problems, we all have to get used to this new protectionist America.

The world's referee has walked off the pitch, to use the metaphor from Chapter 1. The rest of the world must now play on because trade isn't a game. It's the foundation of global prosperity.

This is possible. America accounts for less than 15% of global commerce. The nations that account for the other 85% can guard the rules-based trading system simply by following the rules. And guard the system they must.

The real cost of Trump's Great Trade Hack will come if the system falls. And if that happens, we won't hear a crash – just muffled blows landing on billions of families around the world.

Annex 1: Historical examples of tariffs and industrialisation

President Trump's attempt to use tariffs as a way of driving industrialisation is not original. It's been tried before – so often, in fact, that it has a name: import substitution industrialisation, or ISI.[1]

One of the aims of Trump's tariffs – especially the broad-based 2 April 2025 measures – is to protect US-based manufacturers from import competition in the hope that domestic production will rise to replace goods that used to be imported.

The theory behind ISI is simple. The government imposes tariffs to shield local firms from foreign competition, hoping that this protection will allow them to grow. Build the industries of tomorrow by blocking the imports of today, as it were. But theory rarely survives contact with reality. Or, to paraphrase Benjamin Brewster: the difference between theory and practice is greater in practice than it is in theory.[2]

When tariffs helped industrialisation

Korea's successful ISI strategy

One of the few real success stories is South Korea, which used ISI not as a shield but as a scaffold.[3,4] After the Korean War, the country was divided. Since most of the existing manufacturing base was in the North, South Korea found itself starting from scratch. It exported a bit of rice and tungsten but imported nearly everything else – especially manufactured goods.

Inspired by Japan's earlier experience, Korea turned to ISI. But it didn't just throw up tariffs and hope for the best. It started smart – with labour-intensive light manufacturing that was within reach, both technologically and financially. That worked. Then the government moved into heavy industry, but again with a strategy.

Korea didn't try to build a car industry overnight. It started at the end of the value chain – final assembly – and worked backward. High tariffs and other barriers were imposed on finished cars, but tariffs on parts were kept low. The goa was to make it profitable to assemble cars in Korea. Tariffs on final autos raise the price of cars in the local market by blocking foreign competitors. The higher price on the final autos meant higher revenue to the infant carmakers, and the lower tariffs on the parts keep their costs low.

1   Ferguson, R. W., Jr. (2025, February 24). The intellectual origins of Trump's economic policies. Council on Foreign Relations. https://www.cfr.org/article/intellectual-origins-trumps-economic-policies
2   The original quote is "In theory there is no difference between theory and practice. In practice, there is." Brewster, B. (1882, February). The Yale Literary Magazine, 47(5), 202.
3   Pham, B. (2015). How and why did South Korea transition to an economic model of export-led industrialization? [Unpublished manuscript]. Stanford University. https://fsi-live.s3.us-west-1.amazonaws.com/s3fs-public/2015_benjamin_pham_paper.pdf
4   Lane, N. (2024). Manufacturing revolutions: Industrial policy and industrialization in South Korea (CESifo Working Paper No. 11388). CESifo. https://www.cesifo.org/en/publications/2024/working-paper/manufacturing-revolutions-industrial-policy-and-industrialization

This is the first sign of a critical distinction between final goods and industrial inputs – a distinction that the Trump administration has failed to grasp (more on this below).

In Korea, tariffs were only part of the national industrialisation strategy. The effort was a whole-of-government push: preferential allocation of scarce foreign exchange and credit, training schemes, tax policy, and more.

Korean firms began by importing knockdown kits – essentially entire cars in parts – and assembling them locally. Often the Japanese car companies who sold them the parts would help the Korean firms with some technical and practical aspects of assembly. Once assembly reached scale, the government moved to localise the parts, starting with those easiest to produce. Over time, this deliberate climb up the value chain built a full automotive ecosystem. With state-directed credit, managed exchange rates, and performance-based protection, Korea fostered world-beating firms like Hyundai and Kia.

In a nutshell, tariffs reserved the local demand for cars for Korea assemblers and that attracted supply to the demand. Once there was local assembly, there was demand for parts that where initially imported. The next step was to reserve some of that demand for part for local producers with clever tariffs. And that demand attractive supply, i.e. Korean car part producers. The sequential use of privileged access to demand as means of stimulating supply was what put the "smart" in smart strategy.

But here's the thing. Korea was an exception, not the rule. Countries like Malaysia, Indonesia, and dozens of Latin American countries tried the same model but failed to scale. [5,6] Protection became permanent. Firms never became globally competitive. ISI morphed from a development strategy into a drag on growth.

That brings us back to Trump.

His tariff plan is not part of a carefully designed long-term plan with bipartisan support. The administration seems to be using tariffs like humans in a zombie movie use a machine gun – spray and pray.

There is no focus on technological upgrading. No performance conditions. No coordination across investment, no investment subsidies, and no skills training policy. There was ex ante consulting with American manufacturers, who are the ones who actually know what it would take to revitalise America's industrial base. It's the shallow version of ISI that has failed in country after country.

In particular, the tariffs do not come with a clear, credible, long-term strategy. There is no notion of starting with the production of final goods and then moving up the value

5   Hallak, J. C., & Levy Yeyati, E. (2025, April 14). Failed protectionism: What Latin America can teach us. Americas Quarterly. https://www.americasquarterly.org/article/failed-protectionism-what-latin-america-can-teach-us/

6   Kholilurrahman, R. (2018). Politics of premature deindustrialization: The case of Indonesia [Working paper]. Equality Development and Globalization Studies (EDGS), Northwestern University. https://www.edgs.northwestern.edu/documents/politics-of-premature-deindustrialization-the-case-of-indonesia_robie.pdf

chain. Perhaps worse of all, the tariffs are incredibly uncertain. The administration is flipping between tariffs faster than a teenager browsing on TikTok.

ISI did work for America once before – when it joined the Industrial Revolution after the Civil War. America's own path to top spot on the industrial greatness podium (which it took away from Britain just before WWI) wasn't left to market forces alone. But by the early 20th century, it had become the world's industrial powerhouse. How? In short: protection, infrastructure, immigration, capital, and coordination. It's a great story. [7,8]

America's 19th century industrialisation: Protection with a purpose

After the Civil War, the US was a classic commodity-exporting nation – rich in resources, poor in industry – with the twist that the commodities were in the South while the industry was in the North. And remember, it was the North that won the war.

The Tariff Act of 1864 was the first step. It shielded American manufacturers from foreign (especially British) competition, reserving local demand for local firms. The tariffs were really high and not particularly focused like Korea's, but back then, high transportation costs meant that most manufacturing, final goods and parts, were naturally made nearby. Protecting one protected the other. But tariffs were only part of the story.

The real spark came from railroads – a massive, government-backed infrastructure push that created a vast internal market.[9] Land grants, subsidies, and eminent domain smoothed the way, while the sheer scale of the buildout created extraordinary demand for steel, iron, machinery, and rolling stock. The US laid nearly 300,000 kilometres of track, built 30,000 locomotives, and forged 16 million tonnes of steel.[10,11] With high tariffs in place, this demand stimulated domestic production – not imports.[12]

Meanwhile, a wave of immigrants provided the muscle, the skill, and the demand to drive industrialisation.[13] They filled factories and cities, expanding both supply and demand. And behind it all flowed foreign capital, which brought not just funding, but know-how and technology from Europe. If you squint hard enough while you are looking at this, you can see the outlines of the Chinese industrialisation in more recent decades.

7   Stensrud, C. (2016, October). Industrial policy in the United States (Briefing Note). Civitas: Institute for the Study of Civil Society. https://www.civitas.org.uk/content/files/IndustrialpolicyintheUnitedStates.pdf

8   Bill of Rights Institute. (2024, September 1). The Civil War and the Industrial Revolution. https://billofrightsinstitute.org/essays/the-civil-war-and-the-industrial-revolution

9   Hornbeck, R., & Rotemberg, M. (2025, January 10). Railroads, reallocation, and the rise of American manufacturing. Becker Friedman Institute. https://bfi.uchicago.edu/insight/research-summary/railroads-reallocation-and-the-rise-of-american-manufacturing/

10 Library of Congress. (n.d.). Railroads in the late 19th century. https://www.loc.gov/classroom-materials/united-states-history-primary-source-timeline/rise-of-industrial-america-1876-1900/railroads-in-late-19th-century/

11 Bartholomew, B. (2019, August 2). The steel industry and its place in the American economy. BDO USA. https://www.bdo.com/insights/advisory/the-steel-industry-and-its-place-in-the-american-economy

12 Klein, A., & Meissner, C. M. (2024). Did tariffs make American manufacturing great? New evidence from the Gilded Age (CAGE Working Paper No. 729). University of Warwick, Centre for Competitive Advantage in the Global Economy. https://warwick.ac.uk/fac/soc/economics/research/centres/cage/manage/publications/wp729.2024.pdf

13 Library of Congress. (n.d.). Immigrants in the Progressive Era. https://www.loc.gov/classroom-materials/united-states-history-primary-source-timeline/progressive-era-to-new-era-1900-1929/immigrants-in-progressive-era/

This was America's "big push". It wasn't just about shielding industry – it was about building it, with coordinated policy, strategic investment, and a whole-of-government approach. It worked. By the early 20th century, the US had transformed from commodity exporter to manufacturing superpower.

When tariffs hindered industrialisation

China's path: From supply-chain joiner to supply-chain builder

President Trump's plan to use his 2025 tariffs to "Make America Great Again" is grounded in an old idea – old in the sense of outdated. His strategy for boosting US manufacturing strength comes from keeping foreign goods out and local production in.

But if there's one thing China's rise has shown us, it's that modern industrialisation works differently than when Korea did it. In fact, China's trajectory was almost the mirror image of the old import substitution industrialisation model that worked in 19th century America and 20th century Korea. Instead of building the supply chain from scratch and protecting it behind tariff walls, China joined global supply chains, opening up on both the import and export sides. And in doing so, it became the workshop of the world.[14,15,16]

An important point to keep in mind is that China's industrialisation happened after the global value chain revolution. As mentioned, in the 1990s, the ICT revolution made it feasible for firms in rich nations to offshore parts of the production process to low-wage countries. Final goods could only be globally competitive if firms could source parts and components from wherever they were cheapest. That changed the very nature of industrialisation.

To put it crisply, GVCs killed ISI. That is why China, unlike Korea in the 1970s, didn't try to bring the whole supply chain inside its borders. Instead, it welcomed foreign firms – mainly from the G7 – to set up operations that slotted into global production networks. The government didn't have a detail masterplan. It made China attractive to foreign direct investors, and G7 firms did the rest. G7 firms brought the technology, capital, and knowhow. China provided the labour, infrastructure, and policy stability. It was offshoring that drove the take off – not tariffs. [17,18]

Note that in this join-a-GVC industrialisation scheme, local demand was irrelevant – at least in the early days. China didn't try to reserve its local market for domestic firms, as

14 Baldwin, R. (2024, January 29). China is the world's sole manufacturing superpower: A line sketch of the rise. VoxEU – CEPR Policy Portal. https://cepr.org/voxeu/columns/china-worlds-sole-manufacturing-superpower-line-sketch-rise

15 Brandt, L., Ma, D., & Rawski, T. (2016). Industrialization in China (IZA Discussion Paper No. 10096). Institute for the Study of Labor (IZA). https://docs.iza.org/dp10096.pdf

16 Herrigel, G., Wittke, V., & Voskamp, U. (2013). The process of Chinese manufacturing upgrading: Transitioning from unilateral to recursive mutual learning relations. Global Strategy Journal, 3(2), 109-125. https://voices.uchicago.edu/herrigel/files/2018/07/Final-Reprint-Chinese-Upgrading-1xcl6jd.pdf

17 Murphree, M., & Breznitz, D. (2025). China, global value chains, and the middle-income trap. Business and Politics, 27(1), 1-19. https://doi.org/10.1017/bap.2024.37

18 Parker, B. (2023, September 11). How China is like the 19th century US Construction Physics. https://www.construction-physics.com/p/how-china-is-like-the-19th-century

the US did in the 19th century or Korea in the 1970s. Demand came from exports. Inputs came from imports. China plugged into the world economy at both ends – importing intermediates and exporting final goods. It didn't build the supply chain; it joined it.

But joining wasn't the end of the story. After 2005, China began to shift. It started producing more of the parts it had been importing. This was the move from joiner to builder. The government began nudging firms to localise inputs, investing in infrastructure, talent, and financing. The country started exporting parts and relying less on foreign demand. It wasn't ISI per se – but it was a pivot to building domestic capability, guided by long-term industrial policy.[19]

Over two decades of patient, whole-of-government strategy, China built the largest industrial base in the world.[20] When Beijing decided to push into electric vehicles, production scaled at lightning speed. Yes, China used tariffs and subsidies – but it didn't build its industrial might by blocking imports.[21] It built it by mastering exports, by joining first and then building.

The irony? Much of this was made possible by G7 firms. In trying to cut costs, they helped create their most formidable competitor.

The third phase of the Chinese story is a turn inwards. It is not as widely known as it should be, but China is a pretty closed economy – even when comes to manufactured goods. This is show by the chart below.

CHINA: RATIO OF GROSS EXPORTS TO TOTAL PRODUCTION, GOODS, AND SERVICES

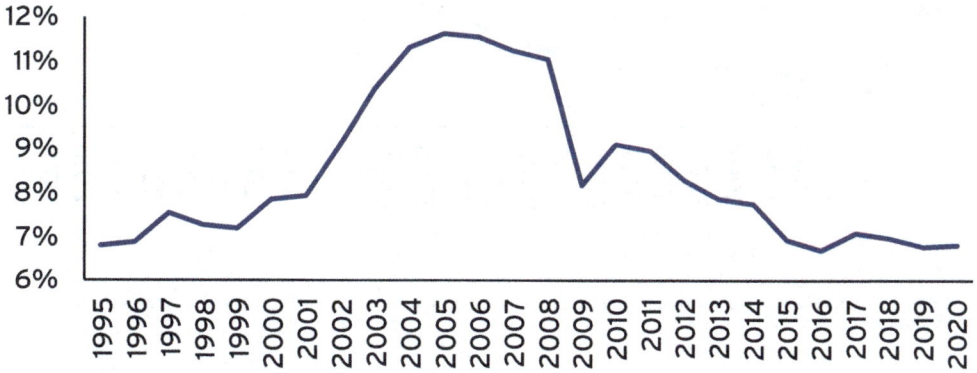

19 Koopman, R., Wang, Z., & Wei, S.-J. (2008). The shifting structure of China's trade and production. IMF Working Papers, 2007(214). https://www.elibrary.imf.org/view/journals/001/2007/214/article-A001-en.xml

20 Wei, J. (2020). China's industrial policy: Evolution and experience (UNCTAD/BRI PROJECT/RP11). United Nations Conference on Trade and Development. https://unctad.org/system/files/official-document/BRI-Project_RP11_en.pdf

21 Rotunno, L., & Ruta, M. (2024). Trade implications of China's subsidies (IMF Working Paper No. 2024/180). International Monetary Fund. https://www.elibrary.imf.org/view/journals/001/2024/180/article-A001-en.xml

CHINA: GROWTH RATES OF GROSS EXPORTS AND TOTAL PRODUCTION, GOODS, AND SERVICES

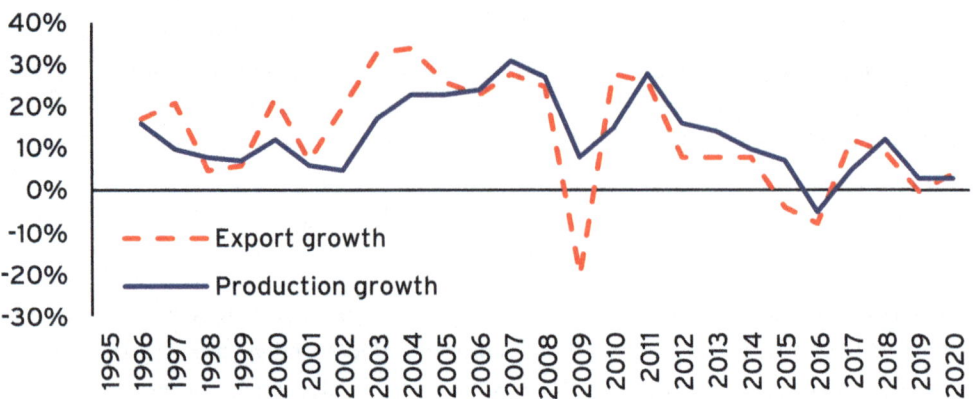

CHINA: SHARE IN WORLD'S GROSS EXPORTS AND TOTAL PRODUCTION, GOODS, AND SERVICES

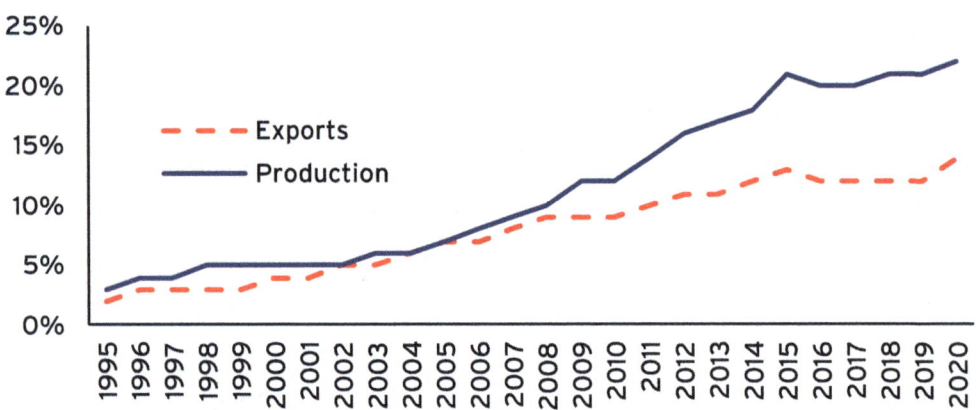

Source: OECD Trade in value added (TiVA) 2023 edition[22]

Note: Calculations are based on the Gross production output and Gross exports. World gross exports calculated as sum of gross exports of all countries in the database.

So, if the Trump administration thinks that tossing around a few tariffs can replicate China's feat, they're chasing the echo, not the sound. And it is a very loud sound that China's industrialisation has made.

China became a manufacturing superpower without tariffs

22 OECD. (2025). Trade in value added: China (People's Republic of) [Data set]. OECD Data Explorer.

If there were any doubts about the success of China's industrial strategy, the scoreboard should clear them up. China is not just a manufacturing heavyweight – it is the only manufacturing superpower.

When it comes to gross production, China's share is three times that of the United States, six times Japan's, and nine times Germany's. Taiwan, Mexico, Russia, and Brazil all now have higher gross manufacturing output than the UK. Canada, once a central industrial player in North America, sits further down in 15th place.

China's industrialisation isn't just large – it's unprecedented. The last time the global manufacturing crown changed hands was when the United States overtook Britain just before WWI. That transition took the better part of a century. China dethroned the US in just 15 to 20 years.

A chart tells the story best. Imagine a 25-lap horserace, one lap for each year of data from 1995 to 2020. China starts the race just ahead of the mid-pack – roughly on par with Canada, the UK, France, and Italy. It passes Germany in 1998, Japan in 2005, and overtakes the US in 2008. After that, it pulls far ahead, while the US and others steadily lose ground.

PERCENT OF WORLD GROSS MANUFACTURING OUTPUT

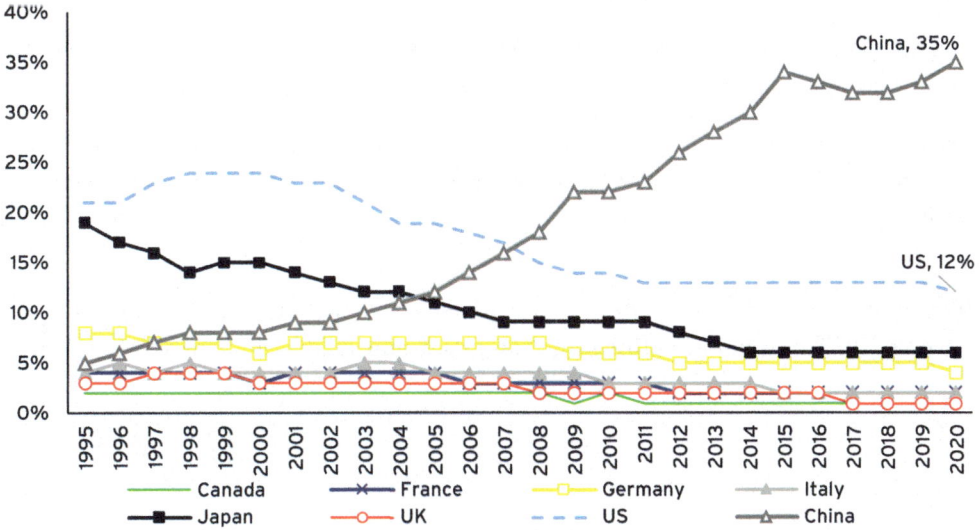

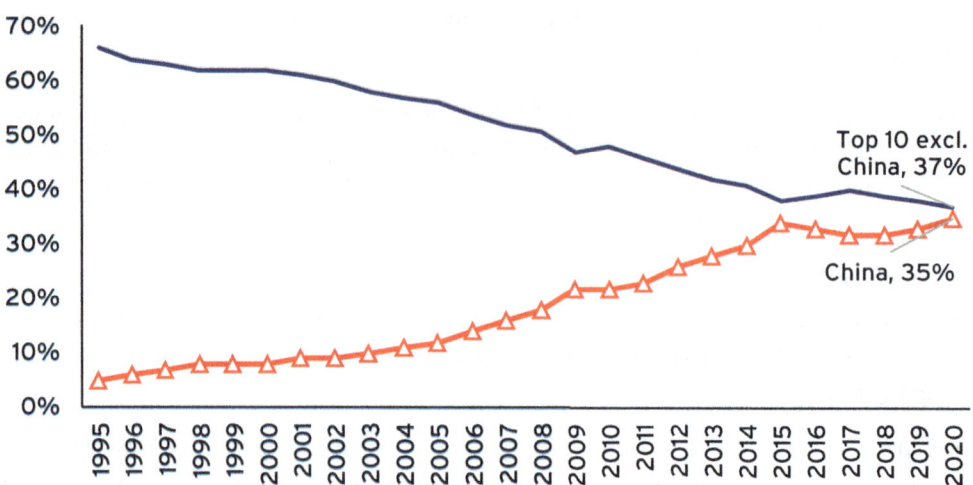

PERCENT OF WORLD GROSS MANUFACTURING OUTPUT

Source: OECD Trade in value added (TiVA) 2023 edition[23]

By the final laps, the race isn't even close. China's share of global manufacturing is close to that of the next ten countries combined. This isn't just a feat of scale. It helps explain the intensity of US–China trade tensions and the global shockwaves when Chinese factories paused during Covid.

India, while not yet close to China, was the second-fastest gainer – adding two percentage points to its global share since 1995.[24]

As of the latest data, China's industrial rise appears to have plateaued, hovering at around one-third of global output. More recent data will confirm whether this marks a peak, but one thing is certain: no nation in history has industrialised faster or on a larger scale.

This is what real industrial strategy – patient, strategic, and state-supported – can accomplish. This is not something that spray-and-pray tariffs can match.

23 OECD. (2025). Gross exports (EXGR), Trade in Value Added (TiVA) database [Data set]. Retrieved May 5, 2025.
24 OECD. (2025). Gross exports (EXGR), Trade in Value Added (TiVA) database [Data set]. Retrieved May 5, 2025.

Annex 2: Two telling examples of exchange rates offsetting shocks that would otherwise be thought to improve the trade deficit

The next example is bit further afield but very telling. It is not about trade policy, but a technological shock that most people would have expected to decrease the US trade but didn't. Macro won and the trade deficit rose. It's a great story. Fracking reduced imports (of energy) but reduced exports (of manufactures) more, so the trade deficit rose.

Example 1: Fracking versus the trade deficit

What if I told you that increasing US oil and gas production harmed American manufacturing? You might be sceptical, but let me explain how this ties into the value of the US dollar and the automatic rebalancing mechanisms that prevents tariffs alone from fixing the deficit.

When US oil and gas production increased dramatically with the fracking revolution, it would have improved the overall US trade balance by reducing net imports of energy[1] – that is, it would have if there had been no change in the value of the dollar to offset the improvement with a drop in exports.

The point is that the US trade balance was in equilibrium before the fracking revolution – in the sense that it matched the economy-wide spending–income gap. Thus, when energy production boomed, the dollar strengthened to restore this equilibrium.[2,3] The dollar's value in terms of foreign currencies rose to the point where exports fell in line with the fracking-induced reduction in imports.

In which sector did the reduced net exports appear? The stronger dollar harmed the cost competitiveness of US manufacturing. This, in turn, led to a deterioration of the manufacturing trade balance.

This narrative sounds fanciful but it happened, as you can see in the three steps and six charts below.

1   Blas, J. (2025, April 13). $50-a-barrel oil is a problem for the US trade deficit. The Japan Times. https://www.japantimes.co.jp/commentary/2025/04/13/world/50-oil-is-a-problem/
2   Yücel, M., & Plante, M. D. (2019, August 20). GDP gain realized in shale boom's first 10 years. Dallas Fed Economics. Federal Reserve Bank of Dallas. https://www.dallasfed.org/research/economics/2019/0820
3   Ricci, M. (2024). The link between oil prices and the US dollar: Evidence and economic implications. ECB Economic Bulletin, 7/2024. European Central Bank. https://www.ecb.europa.eu/press/economic-bulletin/focus/2024/html/ecb.ebbox202407_02~5ce155d504.en.html

Economic mechanisms told through the fracking narrative

Few developments have reshaped the US economy as profoundly as the fracking revolution. It was a true miracle of technology. It dramatically boosted domestic oil and gas production and slashed America's reliance on imported energy.

The funny thing about an economy, though, is that you can't expand all sectors when you're already at full employment. Expand one, and you'll contract another. I can explain in three steps.

The first step is straightforward. With the rapid expansion of fracking from around 2008 onward, US oil and gas production soared (top panel below). This domestic energy boom sharply reduced the need for oil imports (bottom panel below). Exports rose too, but the main event was the drop in imports as this stuff is pretty expensive to move over long distances.

OIL AND GAS EXTRACTION, 1995-2020 (2017 = 100)

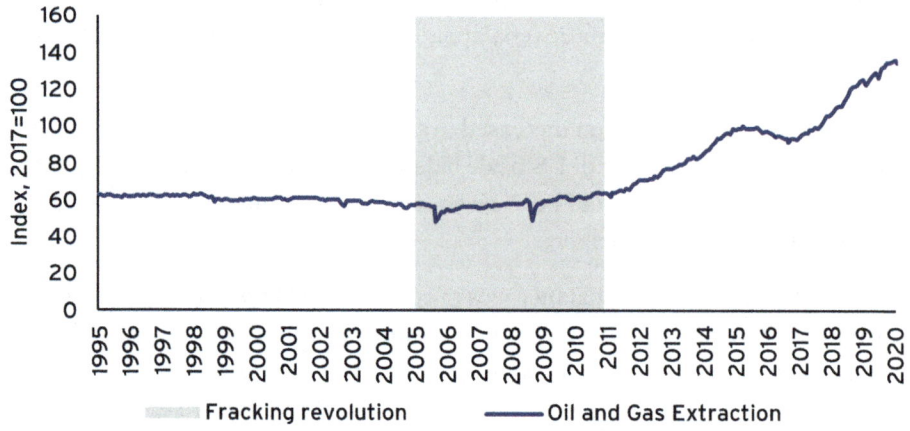

Source: Industrial production: Mining: Oil and Gas Extraction (NAICS=211), Index 2017=100 FRED[4]

4   Board of Governors of the Federal Reserve System (US). (2025). Industrial Production: Mining: Oil and Gas Extraction (NAICS = 211) [Data set]. FRED, Federal Reserve Bank of St. Louis. https://fred.stlouisfed.org/series/IPG211S

EXPORTS AND IMPORTS OF MINING GOODS

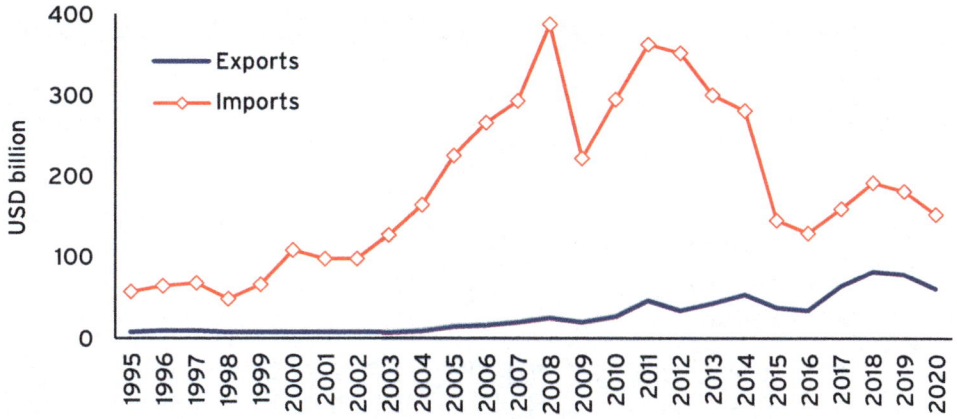

Source: OECD Trade in Value Added (TiVA) 2023 edition[5]

Revolutions are rarely sudden, but 2011 seems a good date for when fracking lit the fuse.

America's trade balance in mining products – dominated by oil and gas – shifted dramatically from persistent deficit toward surplus (top panel below). This sudden turnaround was a big shock to the country's balance of payments. If nothing else had changed, there would have been a large and permanent reduction in the outflows of dollars that used to pay for energy imports.

So, what's wrong with a big improvement in the US trade balance? Nothing's wrong, but it was not sustainable unless fracking had been accompanied by huge macroeconomic shifts inside America. As we have seen, you cannot fix the trade deficit without pulling both the spending–income lever and the relative-price lever. Due to the "secret formula", America's trade balance is slow moving because spending and income are slow moving, at least in most circumstances. Indeed, apart from recessions, where spending typically drops more than income, and economic crises like Covid, where income drops more than spending, both the spending–income and export–import gaps are economic sloths.

To sustain a long-lasting improvement in the US trade balance, US spending would have to come more into line with US income, but that didn't happen. The imbalance levelled out for a few years – and dramatically improved with the 2007-2009 Great Recession – but after that, spending and income continued to get further out of kilter for macroeconomic reasons.

Since the US didn't see the macro adjustment that would have made the net export improvement sustainable, the second step was inevitable: the US dollar appreciated from about 2011 (see the bottom panel below).

5   OECD. (2024). Trade in Value Added (TiVA) Database: Principal indicators, United States, exports and imports, 1995-2020 [Data set]. OECD Data Explorer. https://data-explorer.oecd.org/vis?df[ds]=dsDisseminateFinalDMZ&df[id]=DSD_TIVA_MAINLV%4ODF_MAINLV&df[ag]=OECD.STI.PIE&dq=IMGR%2BEXGR.USA..W..A&pd=1995%2C2020&to[TIME_PERIOD]=false&vw=tb

BALANCE OF TRADE IN AGRICULTURE AND MINING

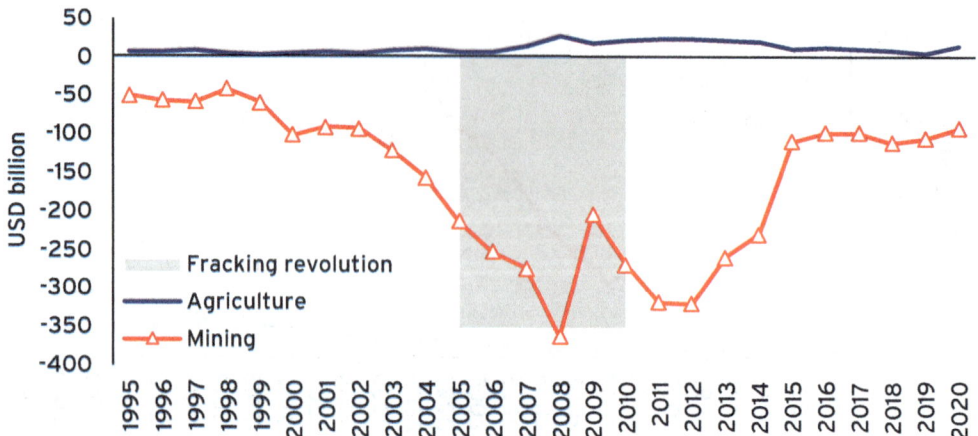

Source: OECD Trade in Value Added (TiVA) 2023 edition.[6]

Note: balance of trade is exports minus imports for each of the sectors - Mining & quarrying and Agriculture & forestry.

USD REAL EXCHANGE RATE (2020=100)

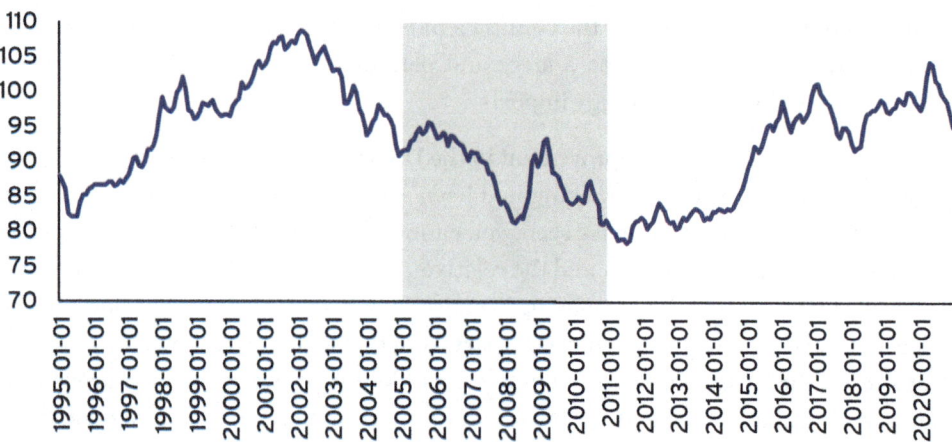

Source: Real Broad Effective Exchange Rate for United States (RBUSBIS), Index 2020=100, not seasonally adjusted FRED[7]

This is expected. This is normal. When a country's trade balance improves substantially - especially due to a surge in commodity exports or a collapse in imports - its currency often strengthens, and that's what happened this time. What is the market mechanism in the foreign exchange market?

Mechanically, the substantial decline in imports of oil meant fewer dollars flowed overseas, naturally causing the dollar's value to rise. A stronger dollar is good for some, but US manufacturers were not among the winners.

This brings us to the critical third step where a strong currency undermines manufacturing competitiveness. As the dollar appreciated, US-made goods became relatively more expensive for foreign buyers, while imports into the US became cheaper for American consumers. The result was as predictable as it was problematic for the manufacturing sector. American manufactured exports stumbled, struggling against cheaper competitors abroad, while imports thrived (top panel below). The manufacturing trade balance began to deteriorate, shifting steadily toward deficit (bottom panel below).

6   OECD. (2024). Trade in Value Added (TiVA) Database: Principal indicators, United States, exports and imports, 1995-2020 [Data set]. OECD Data Explorer. https://data-explorer.oecd.org/vis?df[ds]=dsDisseminateFinalDMZ&df[id]=DSD_TIVA_MAINLV%4ODF_MAINLV&df[ag]=OECD.STI.PIE&dq=IMGR%2BEXGR.USA..W..A&pd=1995%2C2020&to[TIME_PERIOD]=false&vw=tb
7   Bank for International Settlements. (2025). Real Broad Effective Exchange Rate for United States (RBUSBIS) [Data set]. FRED, Federal Reserve Bank of St. Louis. https://fred.stlouisfed.org/series/RBUSBIS

EXPORTS AND IMPORTS OF MANUFACTURING

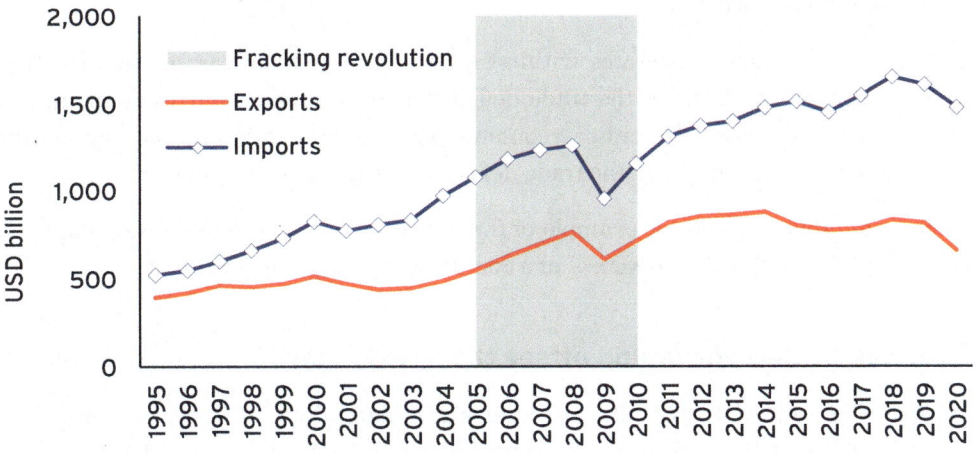

Source: OECD Trade in Value Added (TiVA) 2023 edition[8]

BALANCE OF TRADE IN AGRICULTURE AND MINING, MANUFACTURING

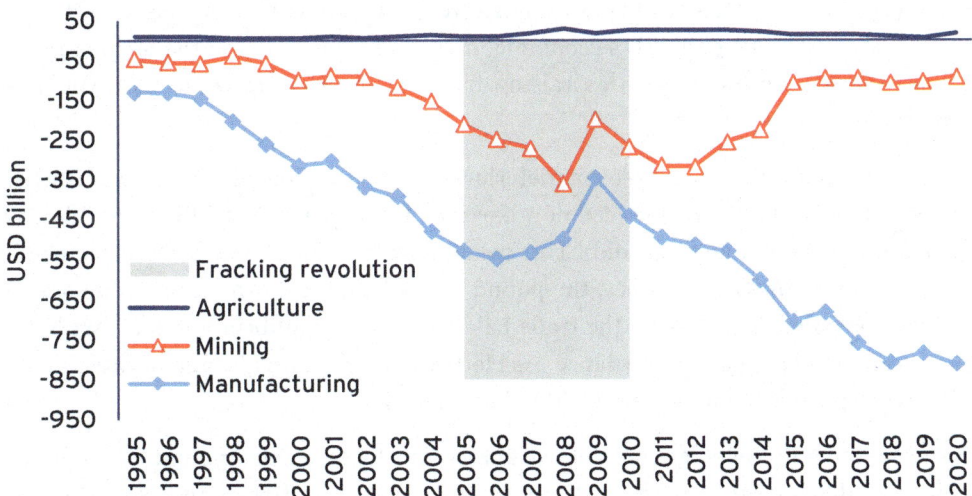

Source: OECD Trade in Value Added (TiVA) 2023 edition.[9] Note: balance of trade is exports minus imports for each of the sectors – Mining & quarrying; Agriculture & forestry and Manufacturing.

Et voilà, as they say in French, that's how fracking hurt manufacturing in the US. The same happened in the Netherlands in the 1970s – which is why this whole chain of cause

8 OECD. (2024). Trade in Value Added (TiVA) Database: Principal indicators, United States, exports and imports, 1995-2020 [Data set]. OECD Data Explorer. https://data-explorer.oecd.org/vis?df[ds]=dsDisseminateFinalDMZ&df[id]=DSD_TIVA_MAINLV%40DF_MAINLV&df[ag]=OECD.STI.PIE&dq=IMGR%2BEXGR.USA..W..A&pd=1995%2C2020&to[TIME_PERIOD]=false&vw=tb

9 OECD. (2024). Trade in Value Added (TiVA) Database: Principal indicators, United States, exports and imports, 1995-2020 [Data set]. OECD Data Explorer. https://data-explorer.oecd.org/vis?df[ds]=dsDisseminateFinalDMZ&df[id]=DSD_TIVA_MAINLV%40DF_MAINLV&df[ag]=OECD.STI.PIE&dq=IMGR%2BEXGR.USA..W..A&pd=1995%2C2020&to[TIME_PERIOD]=false&vw=tb

and effect is called the Dutch Disease.[10] It also happened the UK in the 1990s when the Brits found their North Sea oil.[11]

In short, the US dollar operates within an automatic rebalancing mechanism that ensures any improvement in the trade deficit is dependent on a narrower spending–income balance across the entire economy. This explains why, despite significant changes in energy production, the trade deficit does not necessarily improve.

There is another high-profile example of the exchange rate moving to offset long-term changes in the cost-competitiveness of a country's exports, namely, Brexit.

Example 2: How the pound offset the Brexit "tariff"

With its vote to leave the EU, Britain suddenly, unilaterally, and massively messed up its trade competitiveness with its major trading partner, which accounts for about half of UK exports.

Economic analysts projected that Brexit would act as if a 5% to 10% export tax were imposed on UK's exports to the EU.[12,13] Of course, almost everyone anticipated (correctly) that the UK and EU would sign a free trade agreement so there would be no new tariffs, but leaving the EU's economic integration zone – called the Single Market – was almost universally seen as raising frictional barriers to trade that would be equivalent to an export tax.

Brexit, in short, was a long-term deterioration of the competitiveness of British exports. Due to the Brexit-induced new barriers, UK exports to the EU would decline substantially (and in fact they did). This would have led – had there been no change in the value of the British currency, the pound – to a long-term expansion of the overall British trade deficit. But since the trade balance was in equilibrium to start with, the pound had to depreciate to rebalance. As Herb Stein said, with his famous Stein's Law: "Things that can't go on forever, don't".[14] And they didn't.

Because foreign exchange markets are forward looking, the pound immediately depreciated to offset the Brexit competitive loss. In the first 15 minutes after the referendum results were announced, the pound dropped by about 8% against the euro and the dollar, and it stayed down – settling in at about 9% below its pre-referendum level.[15]

10 Ebrahimzadeh, C. (2003, March). Dutch Disease: Too much wealth managed unwisely. Finance & Development, 40(1). International Monetary Fund. https://www.imf.org/en/Publications/fandd/issues/Series/Back-to-Basics/Dutch-Disease
11 Backhouse, R. E. (1991). North Sea oil. In Applied UK Macroeconomics (Chapter 9, pp. 186-191). University of Birmingham. Retrieved from http://www.socscistaff.bham.ac.uk/backhouse/homepage/aukm/Chapter9.pdf
12 Booth, S., Howarth, C., Persson, M., Ruparel, R., & Swidlicki, P. (2015). What if…? The consequences, challenges and opportunities facing Britain outside the EU. Open Europe.
13 Dhingra, S., Ottaviano, G. I. P., Sampson, T., & Van Reenen, J. (2016). The consequences of Brexit for UK trade and living standards (CEP Brexit Analysis No. 2). Centre for Economic Performance, London School of Economics and Political Science.
14 Stein, H. (1989). What I think: Essays on economics, politics, and life (p. 163). AEI Press.
15 BBC News. (2016, June 24). Pound plunges after Leave vote. https://www.bbc.com/news/business-36611512

DAILY EXCHANGE RATES OF THE EURO AND US DOLLAR VERSUS THE BRITISH POUND

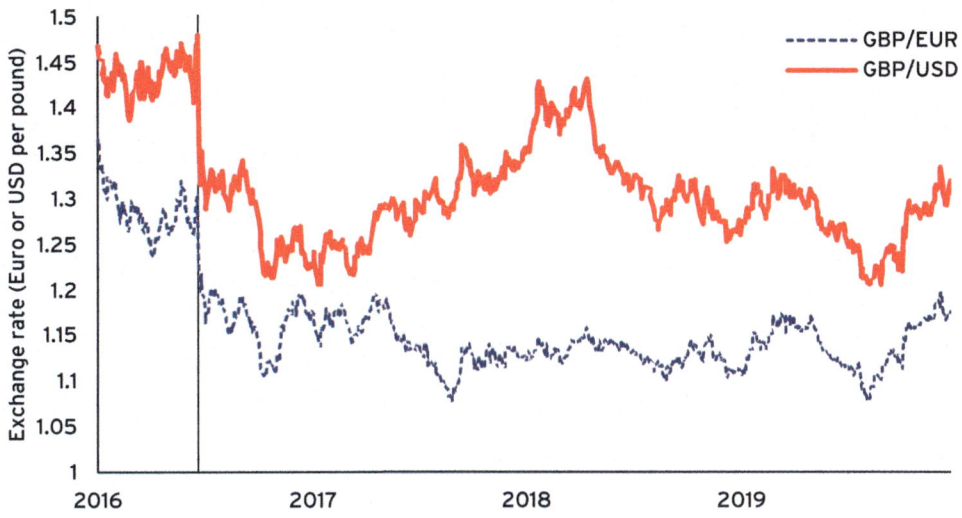

Source: Bank of England[16]

The lesson here is that massive changes in trade policy will be offset by exchange rate movements unless those trade policy changes are accompanied by macroeconomic changes. In this case, the offset came even before the policy change. In the forex game of musical chairs, no one wanted to be the last one standing when the music stopped, so they dumped pounds immediately.

Applying this to the Trump tariffs, it means that the dollar will appreciate, in the long run, to offset its effects on US competitiveness. Well-informed readers will know that the facts of 2025 do not fit this perfectly. The dollar appreciated at first and then depreciated sharply after the 2 April 2025 tariff announcements. Chapter 6 discusses why that is.

16   Bank of England. (2021). Daily spot exchange rates: GBP to USD and GBP to EUR, 2016-2020. Retrieved May 1, 2025, from

Made in United States
North Haven, CT
06 July 2025

70391574R00070